Science ~~WITHDRAWN~~ Fiction Writer's Workshop-I

An Introduction to Fiction Mechanics

BARRY B. LONGYEAR

Owlswick Press
Philadelphia

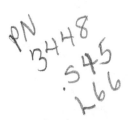

To those who try.

CONTENTS

TABLE OF ILLUSTRATIONS

INTRODUCTION

Most "How To" books on writing fail the beginning writer in one or more of the following areas: not being able to relate to the beginning writer's situation; not being able to make the necessary knowledge understandable; and, last, not providing the direction necessary to develop writing skills to a professional level. To relate to the beginner's experience, you have to experience being a beginner yourself. "Creative writing" texts authored by English academics with little or no freelance experience, therefore, are seldom useful. Even writers with many years of freelance experience sometimes have difficulty relating to the beginner; the bad old times are far behind, forgotten. And why not? Remembrances of those days of panic and nights of gnawing self-doubt—when they would have *paid* a publisher just to see their names in print—are not things to turn to when one needs comfort or security.

Because of that, I doubt that I could write this volume five or ten years from now. My relative newness at fiction writing has left my memories of being a beginner very clear. I can remember making up a new manuscript mailer, with new stamps, simply because the stamps on the first mailer were placed crookedly; and it still isn't funny to me. I can remember my desperate search for an understandable statement of the rules of this business—just what *are* the parts of a story—and those gut-twisting hours before my typewriter staring at blank pieces of paper. But, best of all, I remember exactly what I needed to know to move myself from beginner to professional writer.

For two reasons, I think this book's presentation will be both valuable and easily understood. For the past three years, on a voluntary basis, I have been teaching fiction writing to aspiring writers ranging in age from ten to seventy. Ten-year-olds are not impressed by "ding-words" or writing platitudes; you can't tell them a story needs "polish." Polish is stuff you put on a floor. They want to know *in words* and *by example* what is meant. This required me to do my teaching with a direct, explicit, illustrated approach that has been carried over in writing this book. The second reason I believe this book will be valuable and easily understood is that first draft copies were mailed to magazine editors, writers, writing teachers, a literary agent, and beginning writers for review. Their comments allowed me to clarify confusing areas, present approaches to writing other than my own, and eliminate a considerable number of errors.

Finally, this book does provide direction in developing your writing skills. Do not expect to learn much of anything by giving this workbook only a quick reading. For you to get the most value from this work requires work. Out of the many authors who have discussed their writing approaches with me, few of them think about the nuts and bolts of fiction mechanics while writing a story. All they think about is the story—getting on the paper and fighting it out with the bad guys. The rest is "in their bones." The only time they call upon their knowledge of mechanics is *after* the story is written and it is time to revise and polish up the product. But how did they get it "in their bones?" Throughout this book are suggested exercises and assignments. Only by doing these assignments—in addition to frequent stints at your typewriter—can you become sufficiently familiar with storytelling mechanics to develop the "feel" for a story and how to write one most effectively. The answers to the exercises at the end of each chapter are one of two kinds: either the answer is explicitly spelled out in the previous material, or there is no single "right" answer. Look up the answers that are spelled out. For the rest, find your own answers by writing.

I encourage you to disagree with everything written in this book. Neither this book nor any other work will be the complete answer to you for how *you* must write. That's why being a human is so much fun—and such a bother. We are individuals: unique, animated equations. Only you can decide that which fits within your numbers. However, approaches for story construction, writing, and preparing manuscripts are presented in this book. Not all writers do it the way described in here, but if they *do not,* they usually *do* have reasons for doing otherwise. Do it the way the book instructs unless you have a compelling artistic reason for doing differently. Neither contrariness or laziness are compelling artistic reasons.

THE SF WRITER'S WORKSHOPS I & II

Science-Fiction Writer's Workshop I is the first of two such planned workshops. *SFWW-I,* this volume, concentrates on a general introduction to writing, stressing the short story. *SFWW-II* will expand upon writing for effect—sentence patterns, vocabulary, word usage, transitions, plot structures, scene orders and constructions, characterization, description, dialog, plausibility, and "science"—and will continue by introducing the planning, researching, structuring, and writing of novel-length works. Although both workshops are designed for presentation in conjunction with actual floor discussion sessions, they are designed, as well, for use either as classroom texts or for self-instruction.

ACKNOWLEDGMENTS

There exists a wide body of literature on the how-to's of writing, and petrified academic tradition holds that a proper treatise should contain discussions on all those who went before, the historical evolution of the argument, and exhaustive point-by-point analyses and rebuttals of those aspects of the argument with which the author disagrees. This deck-clearing exercise precedes the author's own views on the subject. Since this is a workbook—not a treatise—and because

I have neither the space, the time, nor the inclination to shovel off this particular deck, I have spared both you and myself this effort. Nevertheless, I must acknowledge the value these earlier works had in the preparation of this workshop, as well as in the development of my own skills. Writing about writing is not lucrative, and the things of value that I have learned have been acquired because many writers took the time to share their views in print. Even those views with which I disagreed were of value, since they forced me to think and to come up with my own methods. The section on references includes a partial listing of these works.

SFWW-I was planned for original presentation at Noreascon Two, the 38th World Science Fiction Convention in Boston, and I would like to thank the convention committee and the New England Science Fiction Society for their invitation. In addition, I would like to thank both the committee and those who attended my SF writer's workshop at NorthAmeriCon in Louisville for the opportunity to demonstrate the interest that exists in this type and area of writing instruction. My reception there makes up no small part of the inspiration and enthusiasm that made this volume possible.

My thanks go, as well, to George H. Scithers, Editor of *Isaac Asimov's Science Fiction Magazine*, both for his help in putting on my workshop effort at Louisville and his ideas, discussions, and encouragement, all of which found their way between these pages. For the chapter on terms, I have borrowed liberally from *Isaac Asimov's Science Fiction Magazine*'s stock of individualized rejection slips, most of which came attached to manuscripts of mine (the rest stolen from George Scithers's office). He should be remembered, as well, for providing most of the editorial rejections and proposing the rewrites that make up the body of this volume.

For their valuable assistance in the preparation of this workshop, my special thanks go to the following:

Beverly Bisbee, Wilton Academy, Wilton, Maine
Mary Ann Drach
John M. Ford
Ron Fortier
Alan Lankin, Assistant Editor, *Isaac Asimov's Science Fiction Magazine*
Adele Leone, Adele Leone Agency, Inc.
Kathleen S. Lynch, Mt. Blue Junior High School, Farmington, Maine
Shawna McCarthy, Associate Editor, *Isaac Asimov's Science Fiction Magazine*
Kevin O'Donnell, Jr.
Claudia Peck
Steve Perry
Darrell Schweitzer, Assistant Editor, *Isaac Asimov's Science Fiction Magazine*
Larry T. Shaw
Stanley Schmidt, Editor, *Analog Science Fiction/Science Fact*

CHAPTER ONE

A FIRST LOOK AT THE STORY

Ever since our fur-clad ancestors gathered around a campfire or huddled in a cave to listen to a story, a "good" story had to contain certain things. What is it that can take a practical, no nonsense, day-to-day type of person (such as our ancestral hunters and farmers were) and have him sitting on the edge of his stump listening to tales of ghosts, impossible heroics, and outrageous superstitions? It is a mystery, except to the storyteller. The storyteller knows that the audience has pains, frustrations, disappointments, crushing doubts, and fears. And the teller of tales knows that the audience is more than willing to trade their lives of mundane, petty evasions for dream worlds of challenge, mystery, and adventure as seen through the mind's eye of the storyteller.

Stories are lies; and the storyteller is a liar. But few think in such terms. Honest, hardworking people sit enraptured, willingly absorbing the lies, finding within them reflections of themselves and their views of the world; right defeating evil, the worth of an individual will, the triumph of justice, the spirits of both man and woman raised above the mean existence of everyday survival. In the storyteller's lies, they find a kind of truth. Perhaps not the kind of truth that is; but the kind that should be. During the story, the truths are lived; afterwards feelings of those truths remain, to be remembered and touched during reality's unceasing efforts to drive men and women into the futile mire of sameness.

There is more that the storyteller knows to make the use of his skill profitable. There must be in the story a being of some sort that the listener can see, can understand, can become. And this being must be tested. Many spend their lives fearing and avoiding tests, confrontations, demands. This is why the creation of the storyteller must be tested, and must rise to meet that test. The courage, the loyalty, the love, the vengeance, and the pain we possess but pale images of, we see resplendent through the special truths of the storyteller. We feel that in some universe—the storyteller's universe—we could be not what we are, but what we *should* be. The storyteller's universe reflects our pain and tells us that we are not alone; it grapples with our doubts and questions and tells us who we are, or who we might become. And this is why, when the storyteller talks, everyone else stops their chatter and listens.

A basic, elementary story follows:

"A STORY"

Once upon a time in a certain place there lived a being who had both strengths and a flaw. This being wanted to achieve a goal. However, there was an obstacle between the being and its goal of such a nature that it attacked the being at its weakest point—its flaw. The being realized that, to achieve its goal, it must overcome the obstacle.

The being struggled to remove the obstacle, trying first one thing, then the next; each time failing—the goal remaining just out of reach. The being at last designed a plan that would make its weakness invulnerable to the obstacle and would, at the same time, achieve its goal.

The plan failed; the being realized its weakness could not be made invulnerable.

The being put on one last, desperate effort to overcome its weakness, and by so doing, the being overcame the obstacle and achieved its goal.

The End

Simply by substitution, thousands of different stories can be told by using the structure above. "A Story" is not *the* formula for all stories; there are many other story structures. However, the tale above does contain *all* of the parts of a story. The main parts of the tale may be organized and labeled as shown in Fig. 1/1.

If we remove the words and leave the labels representing the story parts, we have the structure shown in Fig. 1/2.

Examine and memorize the story parts and the relationship of the parts in the diagram above. To have a story, your manuscript must contain *at least* these parts and in this relationship. This does *not* mean that your story must be written in the *order* described in the diagram. As you will see, there are many ways to arrange the parts of a story. However, all of the parts, and in the relationship shown in the diagram, must be in your story for it to be a story. There must be a character, and the character must be someplace, and must have a goal. This establishes the character situation. Place an obstacle in the path of the character's achievement of his goal. This establishes the character's problem, the main conflict, and story situation. The remainder of the story exists to resolve the main conflict. The buildup is the character struggling to overcome the obstacle. The climax contains the action that resolves the main conflict (either the character achieves his goal or is defeated by the obstacle). This is what you *must* have to have a story.

There is a difference between what is called a story and what is called a "vignette." If all you have is a character in his setting, you have a type of vignette called a "character sketch." If you even go so far as to establish a main conflict, then let your character run around on the paper a bit, but *do not resolve* the main conflict, you have a type of vignette known as a "slice of life." The vignette has its place in literature—even in science fiction—but no vignette is ever a story.

Fig. 1/1 - "A Story" Diagrammed

```
┌─────────────────── STORY  SITUATION ───────────────────┐
│          CHARACTER                                      │
│          SITUATION                     OBSTACLE         ↓
↓   Once  upon a time, in      However, there was an ob-
a  certain  place (set-    stacle between the being and
ting)  there lived a be-   its  goal  of such a  nature
ing (character)  who had   that  that  it attacked  the
both  strengths and   a    being at its weakest point--
flaw (characterization).   its flaw (obstacle). The be-
The  being  wanted to a-   ing realized that,to achieve
chieve  a goal (Motiva-    its goal,  it must  overcome
tion).                     the obstacle (problem).
```

(Main Conflict)

```
┌──→The being  struggled to remove the  obstacle
│       trying first one thing, then the next;  each
B       time failing--the goal remaining just out of
U       reach.
I
L       The being at last designed a plan that would
D  BRIGHT make its weakness invulnerable to the obsta-
U  MOMENT cle and would, at the same time, achieve its
P       goal.

   DARK   The plan failed;  the being learned that its
└→MOMENT weakness could not be made invulnerable.
```

```
┌──→The being put out one last, desperate effort to
│       overcome its weakness (character change),and by
CLIMAX so doing,  the being  overcame the obstacle and
│       achieved its goal (resolution of conflict).
└──→ The End.
```

```
S   CHARACTER SITUATION
T     Setting
O     Character
R     Characterization
Y     Motivation

S
I       MAIN        BUILDUP          CLIMAX
T      CONFLICT    Bright Moment    Character Change
U                  Dark Moment      Conflict Resolution
A
T   OBSTACLE
I     Obstacle
O     Problem
N
```

<u>Fig. 1/2 - Parts of a Story</u>

THE HOOK

The opening of your story should accomplish several things. First, it should capture the attention of the reader, compelling the reader to move on to the next paragraph. Second, the opening should firmly place the reader into the time and place of the story. Special Case: if your viewpoint character doesn't know where he is, put the reader into whatever the viewpoint character *does* see, smell, and hear—what he *does* know or suspect of the when and where of his setting.

The hook sets the effect or "tone" for the story that follows. It should contain action, conflict, drama, or all three. *Some*thing must be happening, and you must convey to the reader that the event is important. Along with what is happening, the reader must know where the story is taking place, at least if the characters possess this knowledge. In science fiction, as well as in fantasy, there is such a wide range of possibilities that you must spell out where and when your story is taking place. *Show* that the setting is Mars in the year 3051 or where/whenever.

If you withhold information from the reader attempting to create an "artsy," "mysterious," or "science fictiony" atmosphere, you will probably create dullness and confusion, but not interest. Readers begin stories for many reasons; few of them begin a piece to be either confused or worked to death. The opening of your story is the piece's first impression on the reader. If it is vague, dull, confusing, or creeping with literary exercises, most readers will believe that the remainder of the story is cut from the same bolt.

Many a reader only looks at the first paragraph of a story, and unless that paragraph has "hooked" him, he will move on to the next story in the magazine or the next book on the rack. Because of the wonderful things that happen later in your story, you might think that such cavalier treatment by readers is very unfair. It is; no doubt about it. Nevertheless, there is a kind of justice to it. As a writer, it is part of your *job* to grab that reader's eyeballs with your opening words. If you fail to do that, you have failed at your job, your craft, your art.

Such failures deserve—and receive—retribution of the worst kind: indifference.

If the chronological telling of your story begins with a situation that compels the reader to move on to the next paragraph, you already have a hook. In addition, you haven't had to rewrite a thing to achieve it. A hook is not to be confused with a "teaser," which is a TV scriptwriter's term for jerking several bits of action out of context and running them before the credits to clue in the viewers that something will be happening later on in the show. A hook is anything that moves the reader on to the next paragraph.

The chronological telling of a story, beginning with the character situation, setting, and so on may be too slow to capture the reader's attention. One way you can develop a hook is to rearrange your story situation. Present the action resulting from your main conflict first, then follow with the rest of the story situation. Another place to search for a hook is in your story's buildup. Take the first buildup scene, move it to the front, then briefly fill the reader in why that situation exists. You can even borrow part of the climax scene, moving it to the front to form a hook (remembering *not* to telegraph the ending of your story). Another way is to begin the story earlier in time: present an action scene that takes place prior to your story situation, then follow with the chronological telling of the tale (see the chapter on "Starts").

BACKFILL

You have presented an interesting opening in your story by pulling an action scene out of chronological sequence and moving it to the front. But the reader knows that your characters were not born at the beginning of your story and that the situation your characters are in had its roots some time in the story's past. In other words, the story situation needs to be established. What to do? Backfill. The purposes of backfill are to explain to the reader why the characters are in the particular situation they are in, to explain your hook, to explain the story's premise, or to provide characterization or character motivation explanations along the story line. There are several methods of backfilling: dream sequences, flashbacks, references, ignorant devices, and parallel running scenes. These are explained in the chapter on "Backfill."

BUILDUP

The buildup of a story depicts the character's efforts to overcome the obstacles between him and his goal. Depending on the length of the work and its treatment, the buildup can take many forms. In a very short piece, the buildup might be a single scene where the character contests the obstacle. In lengthier works, the buildup might be a series of scenes, each scene being a tiny story of its own. You insert bright and dark moments depending on what effect you are trying to create. In any event, the function of the buildup is to lead to the resolution of the main conflict. To maintain reader interest, the closer the buildup moves to the story's climax, the faster and more intense must be the action.

A caution: in stories long enough to contain a series of buildup scenes, a frequent mistake is to make the scene structures the same. For example: character is being chased by a "thing;" through wit, cunning, strength, speed, etc., the character escapes. (Next scene) The character is discovered by another "thing;" but through wit, cunning, strength, speed, etc., the character escapes

Fig. 1/3A Hook: Rearranging Story Situation

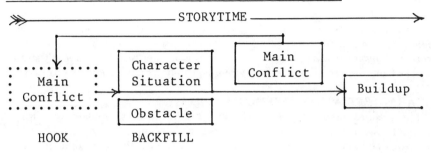

Fig. 1/3B Hook: Moving Buildup Scene

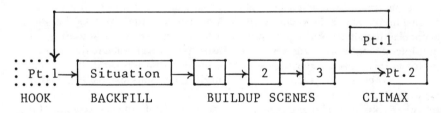

Fig. 1/3C Hook: Splitting Climax Scene

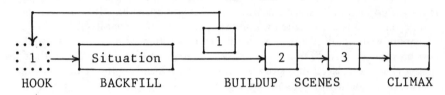

Fig. 1/3D Hook: Moving In Storytime

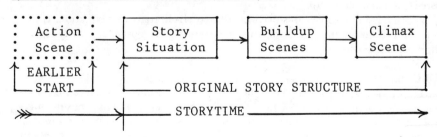

again. (Next scene) The "thing" shows up again, but through wit, cunning, etc., etc., and so on. No matter how exciting your buildup scenes are, repeated scene structures become monotonous.

The buildup of a story must move toward the resolution of the main conflict. A frequent mistake in short story writing is to wander around during the buildup, exploring any interesting situation that presents itself. You can do this in novel-length works, as long as the wandering is interesting and doesn't stray too far from the story line. In shorter works, you don't have the words to spare.

CHARACTERIZATION AND MOTIVATION

The qualities you place in the character or characters that populate your story can make them either heroes, villains, anti-heroes, sympathetic, unsympathetic, or any combination of the above. You *show* the reader a character's qualities by *showing* what that character thinks, says, does, and looks like.

The motivation of a character *is* that character's goals. The attempted achievement of a goal is a factor that determines how and why a character acts in a story. Just as each of us holds many goals—often without recognizing them as goals—so do believable story characters have many goals. For the purposes of a story, one goal is usually the most important to the story character. However, a frequent writing mistake is to put a character in a story who has *only* one goal. You have never met a human with only one goal, and neither have readers. Such a character placed in a story will not be recognized by the reader; it will not convince. On the other hand, some of the best stories that have been written are about characters who hold conflicting goals. Since we have all experienced it, internal conflict is easy to identify with, to believe in.

PLOT

There is one fundamental story plot. A character, against great odds, strives toward a goal and either achieves it or is defeated by the obstacles that have been placed in his path. Every story can be scraped down to some form or multiple of this basic literary equation. Instead of one character, there can be two or more characters striving toward the same goal or toward different goals. Or the two characters each can be striving for mutually exclusive goals: the achievement of one's is the defeat of the other's. Make those two characters each the other's obstacle: a boxing match, with the heavyweight title as the goal. Make a hundred thousand characters the counterpart obstacle to another hundred thousand characters: a battle, with the existence of a nation as a goal. Have five characters struggling against the circumstances of a hostile environment for that precious goal called "life."

Whatever the disguise, all stories are derived from that basic equation. If any function of that equation is missing—character, goal, obstacle, effort, resolution—it is not a story.

CLIMAX

The climax of a story is where the action is the most intense because that is where the main conflict is usually resolved. Notice: *resolved*. This does not necessarily mean that the obstacle to the character's goals has been overcome; all it means is how the story comes out. The obstacle may be such that it defeats the character's attempts to overcome it. The climax of a story usually contains the story's ending (the exception being when a "trailer" is used); and the ending of a story must be the believable consequence of the events that transpired within the tale. The outcome may not be what either you or the reader wanted. Instead, it might be the ending that "had" to be, given the story situation that was created. In setting up a story situation, you are creating an equation of circumstances. As with mathematical equations, there is a "right" answer, and that will be the one that satisfies the reader, even if the answer is not a happy one.

A trailer is a scene run after a story's climax scene. For a trailer to have a purpose, the resolution of one or more secondary conflicts must occur there.

CONFLICTS, PROBLEMS, & PLOTS

Conflict is established by placing an obstacle in the path of the achievement of a character's goal. The character's problem then is overcoming the obstacle. The character's effort in overcoming the obstacle is the plot. A obstacle placed in the path of a character's most important goal establishes the story's main conflict. The character's main problem is overcoming that obstacle. The character's effort to do so is the main plot or story line.

Obstacles placed in the paths of a character's lesser goals establish secondary conflicts; and overcoming these obstacles are the character's secondary problems. The character's efforts at overcoming the obstacles in the paths of his lesser goals are the story's subplots.

CHANGE

As a result of the events that transpire within a story, the character or characters must change; they must be emotionally different from what they were at the beginning of the story. Without this change, the characters in the story become labeled as "one dimensional" or "cardboard." This kind of change is the principal difference between modern science fiction and "space opera." It marks science fiction's maturity as a form of literature and it is a necessary story ingredient.

PURPOSE

What are you trying to accomplish with your story? What is its moral or theme? Is it to demonstrate the worth of a particular brand of morality, to point the way toward the future, to deplore a certain ideology or form of social organization? The story is a lie, but the lie must accomplish something besides simply being believed. It must excite, teach, enlighten, stir to action, soothe, uplift, depress, sadden, bring happiness—*some*thing. Otherwise, there is no point in telling it. And what that purpose is may or may not be your choice. In making up a story, the tale's purpose is not necessarily the starting point. You may not even know the purpose until after you have finished inventing the tale. But there must be a purpose. Without a purpose—or without a purpose of significance—the story becomes trivial.

SCENES

A scene is a unit of continuous related action within a story. A story can take place within a single scene, or it can take many scenes. Usually anything that interrupts the continuity of the story line at any given point—such as a change in time, location, or viewpoint—requires the use of a new scene.

MAKING THE STORY SCIENCE FICTION

There is little that I could write under the above heading that would not be both agreed with and disputed by both writers and readers of "science fiction." Without attempting to placate anyone, I consider today's science fiction a step away from being this age's mainstream fiction. That "step away," however, is a big one.

There is a vast gray area between the two genres that will obtain you "too science fictiony" slips from mainstream publishers and "not science fiction" slips from science fiction publishers—on the same story. I expect this area to expand and to gather both genres under the same "acceptable" label sometime in the future; but until then, use the following criteria: a story is science fiction if one or more of the story elements—location, character, time, premise, etc., —makes the story untranslatable into current or historical terms.

For example, the premise of my Momus stories is the future colonization of a planet by the descendants of a stranded circus starship. The stories that followed cannot be translated into current or past circus stories because two things—the time and the removal of the society from all but circus tradition and influence—permeate every aspect of the stories: the language, the clothing, the relationships, the customs, the institutions, the attitudes, and the values.

In your story, can you replace the blasters with six-guns, the shuttle with a stagecoach, and the hero with Matt Dillon and have essentially the same tale? If you can, it's not science fiction (see Bat Durston under "Terms").

MAKING YOURSELF SCARCE

For a reader to lose himself in a story there are two things that should *not* be apparent: you, the author; and the mechanics of the story. You make yourself the least obvious by showing the reader what is happening in a story, rather than telling (see Show & Tell in Chapter Five). Seams (or joints) occur in a story when the mechanics of the tale (story parts and their assembly) stand out, making the story rough and awkward. For example, your first scene is one of wild combat, screaming monsters, and heroines in distress, followed by a scene calmly recounting how your hero got into this pickle, followed by your hero stepping out to once again do battle with the forces of evil. It is as though you had titled the scenes: "Hook," "Backfill," "Buildup Scene #1," and so on. The main effect this has on the reader is to interrupt the reading flow, making the tale less believable. Seams are eliminated through the use of proper transitions and blending (see Seams in Chapter Five).

SUMMARY

As does a machine, a story has parts, and all of the parts must be there and designed properly for either the machine or the story to work. As with every machine, every story that is a story must have a purpose. The form your story takes will tell its purpose.

The basic story situation is a character, against great odds, facing an obstacle that must be overcome to achieve a goal. The buildup is that part of the story that takes place between the establishment of the main conflict (story situation) and the climax (the resolution of the main conflict).

The opening of a story must establish the story situation. To make such an opening interesting, it may be necessary to pull a scene, or part of a scene, out of the story's chronological sequence and move it to the front. This is one form of "hook." When this kind of hook is used, it is necessary to make clear to the reader why the situation related in the hook exists. This is done through "backfill."

EXERCISES

1. Define the following terms:
    A. Plot
    B. Purpose
    C. Setting
    D. Scene
    E. Characterization
    F. Motivation
    G. Conflict
    H. Problem
    I. Change
    J. Hook
    K. Backfill
    L. Buildup
    M. Seams
    N. Vignette
    O. Subplot
    P. Story Line
    Q. Cardboard Characters
    R. Science Fiction
    S. Resolution
    T. Trailer

2. Outline a story of your own choosing, providing the following information:
    A. Where and when is the setting?
    B. Who is the main character, what characterization has been shown, and how has it been shown?
    C. What is the character's goal?
    D. What is the obstacle in the path of that goal's achievement establishing the main conflict?
    E. What constitutes the story's buildup?
    F. Does the story resolve its main conflict? How?
    G. Does the character change as a result of the events that transpire within the story? How?
    H. Does the character achieve his original goal?
    I. What is the story's purpose?

3. Take a story of your own and diagram it by identifying the story's parts, their relationship to each other, and how they function.

    A. Are all of the necessary parts there?

    B. Did your story establish a main conflict?

    C. Did the conflict resolve?

    D. Is each part developed sufficiently?

    E. Was an effective "hook" used?

    F. What is the story's purpose?

    G. Is the purpose of the story important?

    H. Did the story fulfill that purpose?

    I. Would the story's purpose have been better served by a different arrangement or design of its parts?

    J. If so, what?

CHAPTER TWO

STARTS

The opening of a story should contain the character situation (character, setting, motivation); it should contain action (something must be happening); it should contain conflict (obstacle in the path of the character's goal); and it must "hook" the reader. In other words, the opening must establish the main conflict (story situation), and in doing so, grab the reader's attention. With a short story of 2,000 words, all of this must be accomplished within the first few lines and fully developed within the first page or two. For longer works, a scene might be devoted to developing the opening. A novel may take up to a chapter. Still, no matter what the length, the basic story situation must be established as close to the front as possible.

In this chapter are the openings of several stories, original versions and rewritten versions that sold. In studying these, try to see what is missing in the original versions that is supplied in the rewrites. One of the following openings does not have a rewrite because it contains one of the few mistakes that I haven't made and was written especially for this chapter. Preceding each set of openings are thumbnail introductions. After forming your conclusions about each opening's problem, read the critiques at the end of the chapter.

Introduction:
"The Second Law" was written as the third in a series of seven stories that appeared in the two Asimov magazines. As a general rule, *IA'sfm* does not serialize, but it does like stories with continuing settings, characters, and so on. This requires that each story in such a series stand on its own, in that the reader would not have to read the first two stories to understand the third. What is wrong with the original opening of **"The Second Law"**?

Original Opening of **"The Second Law"**
"A movill for your thoughts."

Allenby held out his hand and Disus dropped a copper into his palm. "I fear I am reveling in the sin of pride, Disus." Pushing back the black and scarlet hood of his magician's robe, Allenby leaned back on the cut stone step of the amphitheater, his elbows resting on the step behind. Disus arranged his own robe, the clown's orange, and adopted a similar posture.

"You have much to be proud of, Allenby. Look at them." Disus nodded at the tiers filling with magicians, riders, trainers, clowns, newstellers, mimes, jugglers, freaks, acrobats, merchants, and artisans. "Masters every one—look! There is Great Vyson of the Dofstaffl newstellers, and look! Great Kamera!"

Allenby smiled, knowing that Disus, a master clown himself, would be staring in adoration at the Great Kamera, master clown and delegation leader to the Ring from Tarzak. . . .

Revised Opening of **"The Second Law"**

As he stepped up the tiers in the spectator's section of the Great Ring, Lord Ashly Allenby paused to listen as a minor poet from Porse rehearsed his argument. The chubby fellow in blue and gray stripes cleared his throat, stood, bowed, and recited:

"We're here to form the Second Law,
    I'm not sure why we do,
The horrors of debate, it seems,
    Not worth the revenue.
Lord Allenby has called us here,
To beg the Ninth to still his fear,
The evil Tenth will soon be here,
    A frightful thing, if true."

As Allenby frowned and took a step toward the poet, he felt Disus, his chief-of-staff, pulling at his arm. He turned and saw the clown shaking his head.

"But, descendants of the circus ship
    City of Baraboo,
I feel I have a question
    I must ask of you:
We've lived here free with but one law
A hundred years without a flaw,
We need another? I say 'Pshaw!'
    And now I bid adieu."

As a few listeners applauded, Disus hustled Allenby to their seats. Allenby sat with a thump and shook his head. "Moon, spoon, June; I hope the armies of the Tenth Quadrant will be amused by the fool!" He pushed back the black and scarlet striped hood of his magician's robe and leaned back on the cut stone step of the amphitheater. . . .

1. Diagram the original opening of "The Second Law."
2. What parts are missing or are poorly developed?

CHAPTER TWO

3. What effect would this have on the reader?
4. Diagram the revised opening of "The Second law."
5. Are all of the opening parts establishing a story situation there?

Introduction:
    "Untitled One" is a bad start opening written especially for this workshop because it contains one of the few mistakes that I never made. Hence I did not have a ready example of this mistake in my story dump. There are, however, numerous examples of this mistake on the newsstands and in beginners' manuscripts. Watch for it.

Opening of **"Untitled One"**
    The winds of the planet Viula were harsh, never ending entities, fleeing from the globe's death-cold poles to meet and clash at the equator where Viula's dim sun would warm them, sending them screaming back to the coldness. The rock and ice of the planet showed paths carved there by the winds, leaving no nook, no cranny, no place of warmth for life to exist. There were the winds, but the sky was always clear. The last snow on Viula fell long ago, before the coldness came, when there was warmth enough for water to evaporate.
    In the sharp clearness of the night sky, stars burned the blackness, rapidly twinkling as the waves of driving wind refracted their feeble beams. At night, against the wind-carved ice and rock, nothing could be seen until Viula's huge moon rose from the horizon—purple, crater pocked, and airless. Its light would cast black shadows upon the surface. Shadows that would move steadily with the motion of the planet in relation to the moon—a phantom army moving without pause toward the enemy of day. . . .

1. Diagram the opening to "Untitled One."
2. What is missing?
3. What effect would this have on the reader?

Introduction:
    The idea for **"SHAWNA, Ltd."** was suggested to me by the Associate Editor of *Isaac Asimov's Science Fiction Magazine,* Shawna McCarthy. She wondered if a story could be written based on the premise that idealist philosophy (reality exists only because we see it existing) works to the extent that it could be used for faster than light travel in space. Instead of pilots, the ship would be controlled by philosophers who would "think" their passengers to their destinations.
    From that suggestion, I invented the "Supraliminal Hegelian Absolutized World Neotranspatial Amplifier" (SHAWNA) Drive. My first problem was making a suitable acronym in honor of the person who slipped me the idea. The second problem was making the premise plausible within the confines of science fiction humor. The usual way to have an insane premise accepted is by "sucking in" the reader (see "Terms"). In the original opening of the story, this is what

I attempted. However, the demands of humor are very restrictive, and I made the biggest mistake that can be made. See if you can catch it.

Original Opening of **"SHAWNA, Ltd."**

Enoch Rawls, PhD. pushed his glasses back upon the bridge of his nose, and peered around the flight terminal. Passengers rushing to and from their flights hardly noticed the old fellow who looked lost in his ill-fitting tweed overcoat, despite the oversized cloth suitcase that threatened to pull his shoulder loose from its moorings. Rawls shook his head and reached with his free hand into his overcoat pocket as the PA system blared departures for New York, Rigel VII, and Andromeda trunk line connections. He pulled forth a piece of paper and tried to decipher his own scrawl. The scribble made out to read: SHAWNA, Ltd. counter, 1 P.M., February 3rd, 2134.

Rawls stuffed the paper back into his pocket and let his gaze wander around the curved interior of the terminal. There was an almost endless succession of ticket counters: TransAm United Airways, British Lunar, Laker Lunar . . . then his glance fell upon the lengthy counter section under the red, orange, and gold sunburst, beneath which a sign spelled out in black sans-serif italic: "SHAWNA, Ltd."

Rawls dodged hurrying passengers and pushed his way through, coming to a stop before a ticket clerk. She wore the company red, orange, and gold over her slender frame, and a badged peaked cap over one belashed eye. "May I help you, sir?"

Doctor Rawls nodded. "Yes. I'm supposed to meet a Mister . . ." He reached into his overcoat pocket and pulled out the slip of paper. ". . . uh, Captain Sanford."

The clerk smiled. "Oh, you must be Doctor Rawls."

"Yes."

"Just a moment, Doctor." The clerk turned and exited through a door. Rawls looked at the passengers lining up at the counter being served by additional clerks. They carried little baggage. SHAWNA Flight 117 was a commuter run—a mere three hundred and twenty light years. Most appeared to be old travelers—already reading papers or magazines, or tapping feet impatiently waiting for their turns. Rawls ran his tongue over his dry lips. He'd never been up before.

"Ah, Doctor Rawls!"

Rawls looked over the counter to see a powerful-looking man with glittering teeth, Hollywood chin, and shiny black hair sporting gray tufts at the temples. "Are you Captain Sanford?"

"Yes." Sanford reached out a hand, grasped the doctor's, and squeezed it with the determination of an apple press. The captain turned to the clerk. "Harriet, be a good girl and take care of the doctor's bag, will you?"

The clerk smiled and fluttered expensive eyelashes. "Of course, Captain. If you would pass your grip underneath the counter, Doctor?"

Rawls flexed his fingers. "Certainly." He pushed the bag through while Sanford lifted part of the counter and stepped to the doctor's side. The captain took Rawls by the elbow and steered him away from the counter.

"Well, Doctor Rawls, I can't tell you how pleased I am to meet you. Doctor Veggnitz, our chief of research, speaks very highly of your work in indefinite propositions and multi-ordinal terms."

Rawls nodded. "Veggnitz was a student of mine." He turned to look at Sanford as they walked. "Will you be conducting this flight?"

"No, Doctor. The captain on this flight is Jerry Wheeler—one of our best. He made his doctorate at Chicago and led his class at philosophical flight school. I'm afraid I'm a little thin on theory, but I can explain the technical aspects of the flight."

Rawls sidestepped a passenger as the two turned and entered an enclosed ramp to the flight gates. The doctor felt the wings of brightly colored insects fluttering inside his stomach. "Tell me, Captain, where did you get your doctorate?"

"Berkeley. Appropriate, don't you think?"

Rawls frowned. "Eh?"

"Berkeley. George Berkley, the father of modern idealism? 'To be is to be perceived'?"

Rawls shook his head. "I don't want to appear dense, but . . ." He shrugged.

Sanford laughed and steered Rawls into a passenger waiting area at one of the gates. "I suppose it's one of our little jokes. You see, Berkley founded the theory, later expanded upon by Kant, Hegel, and Royce, that makes SHAWNA flight possible. And, since I went to Berkeley . . ."

"Yes, yes. I see. What does SHAWNA mean again?"

"Supraliminal Hegelian Absolutized World Neotranspatial Amplifier."

Rawls sighed. "I hope I won't be a dull traveling companion, Captain. I am a semanticist, and I am afraid that much of this is totally beyond me. Forgive me if I fail to laugh at your jokes."

At the rear of the waiting area, Sanford opened a door marked "Crew's Lounge" and ushered Rawls in. Sanford pointed at some chairs. "Please, Doctor. Have a seat."

"Thank you." Rawls lowered himself into one of the chairs and sighed as the weight was removed from his legs. "I'm afraid I'm not used to all this walking."

Sanford grinned. "One of those ivory tower boys, eh, Rawls?"

Rawls smiled sheepishly. "I suppose I am. Theory interests me, but application leaves me rather cold. I suppose it's different with you fliers?"

Sanford nodded. "My meat is action; philosophy in action." He shrugged. "I don't suppose that we contribute as much to the discipline as the theoreticians, but we do make philosophy viable in the marketplace, don't we? If SHAWNA didn't bring in all those passenger credits, who would finance the theoreticians? I ask you."

"Your point is well taken, Captain." Rawls twiddled his thumbs for a bit. "Captain Sanford, as a semanticist I am aware of the vast distance between theory and practice. Yet, Doctor Veggnitz has given me a quite handsome fee to attend this orientation in applied philosophy. He was unclear as to the reason why."

Sanford rubbed his chin and examined Rawls. "Well, Doctor, it's pretty much a company secret. Although they are calling it something else, Air Europe is already utilizing neotranspatial amplifiers. There must be a thousand patent thefts involved, but we have little recourse. Legal tells us that we can't patent the laws of the universe, which is the main thing." Sanford leaned close and lowered his voice. "We have been getting the word for some time now that a line called Trans Galactic will be registered soon, and the only way they can live up to their name is if they have neotranspatial amplifiers as well. Get my drift?"

"I'm not certain. What has this to do with me?"

"Well, Doctor, you are of course aware of the revolution in physics two centuries ago when scientists threw off their Newtonian shackles and brought us to the atomic age. Well, we want to do the same with philosophical transpatial mechanics."

"Perhaps you could explain a bit about how SHAWNA works."

"Of course. First, external objects depend upon mind for existence. This has been known for centuries—the so-called miraculous cures without the aid of medicine, a life completely changed because one believed strongly enough, 'faith can move mountains,' and so on. Even your own discipline provided a thread of the evidence with Alfred Korzybski's theory of the self-fulfilling prophecy: you think disaster will happen, and because of the thought, disaster happens. Am I clear thus far?"

"Yes, I think so."

Sanford cleared his throat. "Well, the inventors of SHAWNA twenty-six years ago discovered the component of mind that contains this power to create and shape reality, and they discovered how to amplify it. Thus, a mind amplified by SHAWNA can, in effect, think itself wherever it wants to go. All that need be done is to proceed on a firm philosophical foundation, dissolve the reality around you, then construct the reality you desire. With the trip we are about to take, for example, the reality of Earth will be dissolved around the ship, and the reality of the planet Betelvane will be created."

Rawls nibbled at his lower lip. "I know flights such as this have been going on for years, but . . . when the reality of Earth is dissolved . . . what happens to those on Earth?"

Sanford chuckled. "Remember, Doctor, there are many minds involved here, each one establishing the substance of its own reality. Those on Earth see themselves here, and see the reality of Earth; therefore, for them, nothing changes. But the amplified perceptions of the philosopher pilots override the perceptions of others about the ship's location. The amplified mind dissolves and creates reality for those aboard the ship. Thus, almost instant travel across light-year distances."

Two flight officers entered the lounge and walked over. Sanford stood and held out a hand toward the taller of the two. "Doctor Rawls, this is Captain Wheeler. He'll be the First Philosopher on the flight." Rawls stood and shook hands with Wheeler. Sanford turned to the other officer. "And this is Lieutenant Valdez, Third Philosopher."

Rawls shook hands and nodded. "I'm very pleased to meet you both."

Sanford turned to the two officers. "I was just explaining to Doctor Rawls about the flight."

Wheeler chuckled. "I hope it wasn't too confusing, Doctor."

"No. No, not at all." Rawls turned to Sanford. "But, I am still in the dark concerning my reason for being here."

Sanford looked at the two officers. "If you'll excuse us, gentlemen?"

Wheeler and Valdez nodded. "Of course. It was nice to meet you, Doctor. We'll see you on board." The two turned and began removing their uniforms as they entered a door marked "Gym." Sanford motioned toward Rawls' chair and resumed his own seat. Rawls sat down. "As I said, Doctor, the company is keeping this under wraps."

Rawls nodded toward the gym door. "What are they doing in there?"

"Limbering up for the flight. The other two philosophers should be along. Even with four philosophers—four, mind you—the demand on the men is severe. And this is only a commuter flight. The Andromeda run has almost as many philosophers as passengers." Sanford shifted in his chair and faced Rawls. "We have to come up with something better, Doctor, if we are to stay ahead of the competition. Longer distances and greater payloads with fewer philosophers."

Rawls rubbed his chin. "And where do I come in?"

Sanford held out his hands. "Doctor, the entire framework of idealistic philosophy is rooted in Aristotelian logic—the old A is A stuff. You are, perhaps, the leading exponent today of Non-Aristotelian logic. Veggnitz hopes that by applying your knowledge and special insights, you can do for transpatial mechanics what Einstein did for physics. You know—soup it up."

Rawls nodded. "I see." He rubbed his hands together. "It sounds exciting."

"It is. Just think of being able to transport megatons of scarce resources from other planets, to bring oceans of fresh water to parched deserts." Two more officers entered the lounge, nodded at Sanford, then headed toward the gym. Behind them, three stewardesses entered. Sanford stood and looked at his watch. "Well, Doctor, I imagine it's time to get you settled in. We'll be traveling in the cockpit along with the crew."

Revised Opening of **"SHAWNA, LTD."**

SHAWNA—(Supraliminal Hegelian Absolutized World Neotranspatial Amplifier) a device that amplifies the component of mind that creates and alters reality. SHAWNA theory, rooted in the works of the early idealistic philosophers, was first made practicable in 2143 by physicist-philosopher Leonid Veggnitz, at which time it was first used in transportation over multi-parsec distances (See SHAWNA, Ltd. under Space Lines, Commercial).

—*Encyclopaedia Galactica*

As the huge, swept-wing liner taxied out to the run up pad at the end of the runway, Enoch Rawls began wishing he had never taken up Leonid Veggnitz's offer. The brain behind SHAWNA, Ltd. had coaxed the semanticist into converting the premises and applications of SHAWNA theory and flight from Aristotelian to Non-Aristotelian logic. "Soup it up," as Veggnitz had put it. The philosopher pilots he had seen in the cockpit looked competent, but Enoch Rawls had never been up before. As the engines grumbled, he turned to his right. Captain Sanford, director of the spaceline's philosophical flight school, looked back. "Is there something the matter, Doctor?"

"Captain, why does this ship have engines? I thought all we had to do was think our way to Betelvane."

Sanford chuckled and nodded his head at the four pilot-philosophers in the seats forward of theirs. "They have to get us into the air, first. Otherwise, we'd leave a dandy hole in the runway. Because of the extra weight we'd pick up, we probably wouldn't make our destination."

"I see."

"SHAWNA flight is limited right now; but as I understand Doctor Veggnitz, he hopes that your work will make us SHAWNA Unlimited—bigger payloads with fewer philosophers."

Rawls nodded and looked toward the front. First Philosopher Wheeler reached to a panel, picked up a mike, and keyed it. "Tower, this is SHAWNA Flight One One Seven, PFR to Betelvane. Over . . ."

1. Diagram both openings to "SHAWNA, Ltd."
2. Do both versions contain complete story situations?
3. Is the revision an improvement over the original?
4. Why?

Introduction:

The original version of **"Project Fear"** never made it out of my office. My wife, Jean, took one look at it, pointed out the problem, then handed it back to me. Through experience, I have learned to take her advice. See if you can tell what the problem is in the original version.

Original Opening of **"Project Fear"**

My first impression of the legendary Red Miklynn was that he was a throwback to the Stone Age who would have looked more appropriate wearing a loincloth and sporting a club rather than wearing terraform greens and group leader's boards. We were in the Terraform Academy's Office of the Commandant. While Commandant Savarat frowned at a pile of papers on his desk, I sat fidgeting in my chair wondering why the commandant had called me to his office. Miklynn slouched in another chair, chewing on the unlit stub of a cigar, legs crossed, cleaning his fingernails with the fifteen-centimeter-long cutter of a switchblade knife.

Commandant Savarat looked up at Miklynn, glared for a moment, then returned his attention to his papers. Although Miklynn never looked up from his fingernails, I saw him grin around his cigar. "Is it gonna be much longer, Savarat?"

He called him "Savarat." Not commandant, not sir, just Savarat. The commandant's cheek muscles twitched. He took two deep breaths, then looked at me as though by directing his answer toward me he avoided answering Miklynn. "Dean, Mr. Lua of the Arapeth Department of State will be here any moment."

I half opened my mouth to speak, but Miklynn closed the blade on his knife, slipped it up his sleeve, then grinned at the commandant. "No hurry. Just curious." He turned his short-cropped bullet head in my direction. "What year're you in, kid?"

I looked at the commandant, then turned back to look at Miklynn. "I'm a senior."

"Specialty?"

"Alien psych."

Miklynn nodded, then fixed me with the brightest blue eyes I had ever seen. I half noticed that his lashes were white. "You're not a garry or a Christer, are you?"

My mouth fell open as I looked at the commandant, his face now buried in his papers. I looked back at Miklynn. Behind him, on the wall, was a two-meter-high poster proclaiming the eternal nondiscrimination of the Terraform Corps, and that beer-gutted pig had just asked me whether I was a homosexual or a religionist! My mouth was still hanging open when the commandant's door opened behind us. I turned and saw an unimpressively built creature standing one and a half meters tall, almost completely covered with long blond hair. "Commandant Savarat, your aide told me to go right in."

The Commandant and I came to our feet while Miklynn turned his head and faced the creature with a bland expression. The commandant held out a hand in my direction. "This is Kevin Dean, a senior here at the Academy." He moved his hand to point at Miklynn. "And this is Group Leader —"

Miklynn held a hand up. "No need to introduce us, Savarat. Lua and I are old friends." Miklynn lowered his hand, spat a flake of tobacco on the commandant's spotlessly polished floor, then looked at Lua with narrowed eyes. "How's it hanging, Lua?"

The creature tossed a mass of hair aside, exposing a reddish face with solid black eyes. He looked at the commandant. "Commandant

Savarat, I have agreed to the employment of Group Leader Miklynn, but I fail to see the need for us ever to meet!"

Miklynn turned toward me and raised his brows. "You see, kid, after I completed the troubleshooting on one of Lua's planets, this hairball told the Corps that he never wanted to see me again." He looked back at Lua. "In fact, he demanded my discharge from the Corps; and got it, too." Miklynn reached up a beefy hand and brushed imaginary dust from his group leader's boards.

Commandant Savarat cleared his throat. "I'm certain that your little . . . misunderstanding with Mr. Lua has been cleared up."

Miklynn's eyes never left Lua. "How about it, hairball? Is our little misunderstanding cleared up?"

Lua's dark eyes flashed. "Miklynn, I realize that—for the moment—I am in need of your peculiar skills. But there will come a time . . ." Again the commandant cleared his throat. "Gentlemen, if we could be seated?" Mr. Lua walked behind me and took a chair to the left of the commandant's desk. "Now, gentlemen, please forgive me if I conduct these negotiations with an unusual degree of clumsiness. Usually Marshal Decker would conduct them, but it seems—"

Miklynn chuckled and shook his head.

"—it seems that the Marshal had another commitment."

Lua snorted. "You mean that Decker cannot stand the sight of Miklynn any more than can I."

Savarat's lips twitched as his face grew red. He cleared his throat, then picked up a sheaf of papers and handed them to Mr. Lua. "This is the contract. Read it and sign it."

Lua reached out a hairy, claw-covered hand, snatched the papers from Savarat, then began working his way through the pages. Miklynn held out an open hand toward the commandant. Savarat raised his brows. "What is it, Miklynn?"

Miklynn grinned. "The contract. Let me see a copy."

"You are an employee, Miklynn. The Arapeth Council, who Mr. Lua represents, has contracted with the Corps—not with you."

Miklynn's hand remained out. "Thanks to Lua—and a few of you armchair pilots in the Corps—it's been a long time since I've seen a Terraform Corps contract." He snapped his fingers. Savarat drummed his fingers upon another sheaf of papers, then lifted the contract copy and handed it to Miklynn, who immediately began highspeeding the sheets. I turned to face the commandant.

"Sir?"

"*What!?*" Savarat's face again turned red. "I apologize, Dean. What do you want?"

I swallowed. "Sir . . . why am I here?"

The commandant slumped back in his chair. "Alien psych specialists are fairly scarce, and . . . Miklynn requested one from the Academy for the D'Maan job. If you and Miklynn find each other acceptable—" he snorted "—the Academy will graduate you early . . ."

Revised Opening of **"Project Fear"**

The blood streams down my face, drips from my hands as though they had been dipped into scarlet paint. "This is not real!" Why can't I hear myself? These dark, twisted trees, that sky of boiling fire; where is the beautiful planet? "Is anyone alive?"

Arango's uniform slumped up against a slime-covered rock, the naked skull above it grinning while a finger-thick worm crawls into one eye socket, then exits through the other. Parks' remains lay scattered upon the spongy soil. The creatures had eaten their fill while Parks still lived. Gorged, the things then played with Parks, tearing at him until he died, ending the creatures' interest. Jerzi Nivin sat, watching his legs dissolve. "The real," I shrieked, "show me the real!"

"Dean!" I turned, wiped the blood from my eyes, and saw Miklynn. He wrung his hands as the tears dribbled down his cheeks. "Dean, for god's sake! Stop this! Stop it!"

"No!" I stumbled toward the pool, then stopped at its edge. The image of the surface swam before my eyes as I concentrated on what I knew had to be. I drove time back, swearing, hoping, praying. Miklynn . . . got to . . . think. Got to concentrate on Miklynn . . .

My first impression of the legendary Red Miklynn was that he was a throwback to the Stone Age . . . [and so forth, continuing with the original opening].

1. Is a complete story situation set up in the original version?
2. If so, what's wrong with it?
3. What is the purpose of the change in the revised version?

Introduction:
"The Magician's Apprentice" was written as the second in the series of seven "Momus" stories mentioned in the introduction to "The Second Law." The problem with this story was partly the same as the incomplete story situation of "The Second Law." However, a rewrite was requested on "Apprentice" for reasons similar to the problem with "Project Fear." The problem, however, could not be solved in the same manner. See if you can tell what I did.

Original Opening of **"The Magician's Apprentice"**

Crisal, still smarting from her father's words, looked nervously at the great magician's door. Its black and scarlet striped curtain hung motionless in the noon sun, while the reflection from the whitewashed adobe hurt her eyes. A decision made, she clenched her fists, arms held straight at her sides, and marched through the door. She found herself standing next to a tall barker, dusty and smelling of the road. Across from the barker, a tiny old man garbed in black and scarlet robe sat on a low stool, his gnarled hands supporting him by gripping an equally gnarled staff. The old man nodded at the barker.

"A moment, Yudo, while I find out who my hasty visitor is." The old man raised his eyebrows at the girl.

"Fyx, I am Crisal. I, I didn't know you had company."

"I suppose, Crisal, it would have been too much trouble to call to the house. Never mind, little fortune teller. What brings you?"

"Fyx, I would be a magician."

The old magician looked the girl over from the top of her unkempt tangle of red hair to her dusty bare feet. "First, you are a girl; second, you are obviously of the fortune tellers; third, you are rude. Why should I apprentice you to the magician's trade?"

"First, Fyx, women have been magicians before. Myra of Kuumic played the Great Square here in Tarzak only yesterday."

The old man nodded. "Rare, but it has been done. But Myra is the daughter of a magician. Explain that blue robe you wear—at least I think it is blue under all that dirt."

"I am of the Tarzak fortune tellers. My mother is Salina. I told her as I tell you, I *choose* to be a magician. I have completed my apprenticeship; no one can force me to be a fortune teller." Crisal folded her arms, her nose in the air.

"Salina, eh?" Fyx scratched his head, then rubbed his chin. "You say you told this to Salina?"

"Aye."

"And what did the Great Salina say to you?"

"She said my life was my own and to do with it what I choose."

The corners of Fyx's mouth went down as his eyebrows went up. "She did? And your father, Eeren?"

Crisal frowned. "He was not understanding."

"I see. Now, about the third thing: your rudeness. Not even my own sons addressed me simply as 'Fyx.' "

Crisal cocked her head to one side. "You insist?"

The old man nodded. "Try it once."

The girl bowed, loading her voice with sarcasm scraped from the floor, "*Great* Fyx."

"I see your respect would be more of a burden to both of us than your rudeness. And, now for the important part. Why should I take you on?"

Crisal smiled. "I know how you do your trick of the missing card."

The old man nodded, smiled and pointed to a cushion next to his table. "Sit there, Crisal, and we will talk later. I don't want to hold up my visitor's business any longer." Walking in front of the barker, Crisal approached the table and sat upon the designated cushion.

The barker bowed. "Great Fyx, is this something to say in front of the child?" Yudo pointed at Crisal.

Fyx looked at her, then turned back to the barker. "The little beast is my apprentice, Yudo. She is held under my vow of confidence, which is something she *will* respect!" Fyx turned back to the girl. Crisal nodded and smiled.

Yudo shrugged. "As you say, Great Fyx. Will you come to Ikona?"
Crisal saw fear in the barker's eyes, but it was not fear of Fyx.

"And you say the fee is twenty thousand movills?"

"In advance." Yudo pointed at the stack of bags on the floor.

Fyx nodded. "A handsome sum. We were interrupted before you said
what I must do for it."

"Ikona is a farming village, Great Fyx, and our crops die—"

Fyx held up his hand. "Save your coppers, Yudo. I am a magician,
not a farmer."

"The crops die, Great Fyx, because of a magician. Rogor, the Black
One."

"Rogor . . . I have heard of this one, but he calls himself a sorcerer,
not a magician."

Yudo bowed his head. "You all call upon the same dark spirits. Ikona
has no place else to turn for help." The barker reached into his robe
and brought forth an envelope. "The Dark One made this appear at
the fountain in Ikona. It is addressed to you."

Fyx opened the envelope and squinted at the sheet of paper inside.
Lifting his head, he turned to Crisal. "Fortune-tellers do not read, do
they?"

"I do."

Fyx held out the letter. The girl stood, walked to the old magician,
and took the letter. "Read it aloud."

Crisal held the letter to the light and began: "To Fyx, ancient and
worthless patriarch of the Tarzak Magicians, Greetings. A fool from
Ikona will ask you to come and do battle with me in my Deepland
kingdom. He is a fool because he asks you; you are the bigger fool if
you accept.

"Stay in the city, carnival trickster, and stay safe. In the Deeplands,
I rule without challenge, for I have the power of Momus at my hands."
Crisal looked at Fyx. "It is signed 'Rogor' in a strange way."

"Strange how?"

"In a cross; look."

Fyx looked at the bottom of the sheet and saw the signature in bold
letters:

<pre>
          R
          O
      R O G O R
          O
          R
</pre>

"What does it mean, Fyx?"

The magician frowned. "It is a palindrome; a word that reads the
same frontwards or backwards. Other than that, it means nothing."

Yudo shook his head. "Great Fyx, it is the Dark One's sign. Show disrespect to it in Ikona and your crops die. You must then pay Rogor to leave you be."

Fyx looked at a dark spot on the ceiling. ". . . ancient and worthless patriarch . . . ." He turned his gaze on the barker. "Yudo, you fool, a bigger fool accepts your offer. Tell that to Rogor."

"I cannot. No one knows where Rogor lives."

Fyx shrugged. "How then am I supposed to do battle with the fumble fingered Dark One?"

Yudo trembled. "Please, Great Fyx. Express your discourtesies after I have left." The barker bowed and backed out through the door. Fyx looked into Crisal's eyes.

"In the barker's eyes, what did you see?"

"Fear. As though Rogor could reach down and pluck him from your house if he chose."

The old magician nodded. Standing, he hobbled over to a chest, opened it and pulled out a black and scarlet robe. He handed it to the girl. "Wash, then put this on. There is a pool in back of the house. We will leave before light tomorrow for the Deeplands."

Revised Version of "The Magician's Apprentice"

Yudo and his two brothers stood looking at their grain field. Green only the day before, it now lay brown and withered. Yudo nodded. "It is the power of Rogor. Your tongue angered him, Arum."

"Bah!" Arum bent over and pulled up a handful of the brown plants, then held them over his head. "Rogor! Since the circus ship brought our ancestors to Momus, we have served no man—"

"Arum!" Yudo held up his hands and looked with horror at his brother Lase.

Lase stood next to Arum and grabbed his arm. "Would you bring down more of this upon us?"

Arum shook off his brother's hand. Throwing the withered plants upon the ground, Arum turned to his two brothers. "A fine pair you make. Look at you shaking in your sandals."

Lase wrung his hands, looked to Yudo, then back at Arum. "We are barkers by tradition, Arum. Perhaps we should go to Tarzak and be barkers again."

Arum shook his head. "As I said, a fine pair." He held out his arms indicating the fields belonging to the three. "After all of our work you would have us fetch and carry pitches for others?" Arum put his hands on his hips. "We are men of property. No carnival trickster will change that—"

Lase and Yudo watched as Arum grabbed at his own face while his red and purple striped robe burst into flames. In seconds Arum lay dead, his body burned beyond recognition. Then the body disappeared.

"Arum!" Yudo took a step toward the spot where his brother had been standing, but stopped as a figure clad in black and scarlet appeared on the spot. Its face was hidden by a hood. "Rogor!"

The figure pointed at Lase. "Arum offended me. Do you believe as he believed?"

Lase clasped his hands together and bowed. "No, Great Rogor! Spare me!"

"Lase, you would do my bidding?"

"Yes, Great Rogor."

"Then go to all the towns in Emerald Valley and tell them to go to Ris. They are to wait there until I appear."

"Yes, Great Rogor."

"Then go." Lase looked at Yudo, back at Rogor, then began running across the field toward Ikona. Rogor turned toward Yudo. "For you, barker, I have an important task. Go to the fountain in Ikona. Your instructions are there." Yudo closed his eyes and nodded. When he opened them, Rogor was gone.

Eight days later, far to the south in Tarzak, a young girl looked nervously at a great magician's door . . . . [and so on, continuing with the original opening].

1. What is the similarity of problems between the original openings of "Project Fear" and "The Magician's Apprentice"?

2. The problem was corrected differently in "The Magician's Apprentice." How was it corrected?

CRITIQUES

"The Second Law"

The original version of this opening is very confusing—almost incoherent—to any reader who hasn't read either of the preceding stories in the series. Virtually all of the parts that make up the story situation are missing. Who are these people? Where are they? Why are they there? Why are they dressed in costumes? What is a Ring? What are the character goals? What are the obstacles to those goals? What is the main conflict? The original version supplies none of these answers until much later in the story.

Fig. 2/1, Original Opening to "The Second Law"

```
CHARACTER SITUATION
  Setting: an amphitheater (where? when?)
  Character: Allenby
  Characterization: (tired? bored? smug?)
  Motivation: ?
                  NO MAIN CONFLICT ESTABLISHED
OBSTACLE: ?
```

When I wrote the original version of this opening, the answers to the questions above were very clear to me because I had stated the story situation twice before in "The Tryouts," and "The Magician's Apprentice." No reader who had read those two stories would have been lost by the original opening. However, that is *not* what is meant by a story being complete or "standing on its own." The story cannot depend upon other stories to make itself clear.

The rewritten version, through the character of the poet and Allenby's reaction to the poet, answers the questions. Who are these people? They are the descendants of a wrecked circus starship, and it can be inferred that they are in costume because that was the way the society developed. The Great Ring—an amphitheater—makes sense now, because we are all familiar with circus rings. They are gathering there, at Lord Ashly Allenby's request, to consider the formation of a law to seek protection from the "armies of the Tenth Quadrant" by requesting Ninth Quadrant intervention. The passage of this law is Allenby's obvious goal, and the apparent indifference of the delegates to the law is the obstacle establishing the story's main conflict and story situation.

Fig. 2/2, Revised Opening to "The Second Law"

CHARACTER SITUATION
   Setting: The Great Ring, planet Momus,
          100 years after passage of the First Law
   Character: Lord Ashly Allenby
   Characterization: Quick to anger, but restrained
   Motivation: To get the inhabitants of Momus to pass
          the Second Law, requesting Ninth Quadrant
          protection against the designs of the
          Tenth Quadrant's armies.

                        MAIN CONFLICT ESTABLISHED
OBSTACLE
   Obstacle: The Momans are indifferent to the threat
   Problem: To change the Momans' attitude

Allenby's behavior in the original version is weariness, which would have been clear to those readers familiar with the trials Allenby had endured to get the people to gather and consider the passage of the law. However, without this knowledge, Allenby's behavior in the original version can be easily mistaken for amused indifference. In other words, it would appear that nothing of importance to anyone is happening. Allenby's anger in reaction to the poet's argument in the rewritten version establishes the importance of the goal to Allenby, not to mention the importance of the threat to an innocent, uncaring population.

"Untitled One"

Fig. 2/3, Opening to "Untitled One"

```
CHARACTER SITUATION
  Setting: the planet Viula (when?)
  Character: ?
  Characterization: ?
  Motivation: ?
                            NO MAIN CONFLICT ESTABLISHED
OBSTACLE:?
```

This opening is a travelog—a solid hunk of description—not a story situation. None of the parts that constitute a story situation, except for a setting, are there. They can't be because the opening contains no character. Without a character there can be no goals, obstacles, conflicts. The reason I never made this mistake in my writing is because I never liked reading or writing blocks of description. During such moments, the author may be having a lot of fun, but the story is racing its motor waiting for the author to get it in gear. This applies as well to blocks of character description. Nothing happens while the author practices expository description exercises. No matter how well the description is done, the story is not moving. There are readers who will sit still for almost anything, including blocks of excellently executed description. However, many readers won't, particularly if it takes place at the opening of the story, giving the tale a slow start.

Providing that the description contained in the opening is necessary to the story, instead of presenting it in a hunk at the opening, it would be better to precede it with a scene establishing the story situation. Even better would be to break up the description into parts and mix those parts with the scene establishing the story situation. As is a general rule, only describe it when it is doing something, or when something is being done to it (such as a character looking at it).

"SHAWNA, Ltd."

Both openings to this tale contain complete story situations. A character (Enoch Rawls) has been presented, in a setting (Earth, 2143), and the character has been faced with a problem ("souping up" SHAWNA flight). Characterization has been provided (Rawls is a mousy, frightened semanticist) and the nature of the obstacle has been explained (SHAWNA flight and the improvements in it expected by Veggnitz from Rawls). Why is the revised version an improvement upon the original?

The editorial comment from *IA'sfm* on the original version contained the following: ". . . it starts slowly. It needs tightening up by perhaps as much as a third, all in the first half. . . . There is a bit much lecture here." From the table of terms you will recall that "slow" means that the number of words per significant event taking place is too high. "Tighten up" means to get from A to B by a more direct route. To accomplish the same thing, the original version took 2,200 words, while the revised version took 350 words. In other words, the first strike against the original opening as a piece of humor was that it was too long (the entire piece ran only 5,000 words in the original version; 3,100 in the rewrite). The biggest mistake one can make in humor is to make it boring—exactly what I accomplished with the original opening.

The original reason for the spaceline terminal scene, with Sanford, the philosopher pilots, and Rawls talking matter-of-factly about SHAWNA flight, was to "suck in" the reader. I was trying to make the premise believable. However, in so doing, I also made it very boring (lectures: see "Terms" and Captain Sanford's mouth exercises in the original version of the opening. Also, this story's section in the chapter on "Backfill"). But, how to throw out a third of the story (all at the opening) and still "suck in" the reader?

I got the idea for the story from someone at Davis Publications; therefore, I ripped off another idea from someone in the same employ to save my story: Isaac Asimov's *Encyclopaedia Galactica*. If you can't trust the *Encyclopaedia Galactica*, what can you trust? Insanity in print becomes authority. A citation, even from a fictional reference, lends a great deal of credibility to a premise. Any reader who wouldn't go along with the premise as presented in the *Encyclopaedia* certainly wouldn't accept it as presented in the unbearably-drawn-out original opening. In the revised version, after the citation, we find Enoch Rawls in the cockpit, facing the problem. The story is moving, right from the beginning.

"Project Fear"

The original version of "Project Fear" was a straight chronological relating of the events in the story. As is frequently the case with such presentations, the story lacked a compelling "hook." That was what my wife saw immediately. I then went searching along the story line for a scene with enough dramatic impact to serve as a hook. "Project Fear," however, had special problems. The first scene set up the story situation, followed by twelve buildup scenes, climax and trailer. The story takes Kevin Dean from the Academy, introduces him to the other members of the troubleshooting crew, then begins investigating the peculiar problems of the planet D'Maan. It is a visually beautiful planet, but none of the several troubleshooting teams that have touched down on the planet's surface before have ever survived. The buildup continually moves the characters closer to a confrontation with "the thing," but to maintain the contrast between the beauty of the planet before meeting "the thing," and the horror of it after meeting "the thing," the entire length of the buildup was low keyed and had nothing that could be extracted as an effective "hook."

The first moment of startling drama in the original version was in the climax scene. Pulling that scene and moving it to the front of the story would have provided an effective hook, but it would have left me with nothing but backfilling for the rest of the story. Instead, I divided the climax scene, moving part of it toward the front for a hook. The story now had a hook and was mailed off. However, the editor telephoned me and gave me the unhappy news that, because of the number of characters in the story, none of them were very well developed. Develop them. What to do, what to do? Dumping stretches of characterization on my already low-keyed buildup would make the body of the story very tiresome. See Chapter Three, "Backfill," for what I did.

"The Magician's Apprentice"

This story had a "saga" presentation, in that it was a chronological presentation of the events in the story. The editorial comment regarding this piece was that it needed to get off the ground faster. It had a slow start. There was no way to pick out something from the story line for a hook; doing so would have destroyed the effect I was trying to create by signaling the nature of the story's climax. Instead I moved forward in story time and created the scene with Yudo and his two brothers. This accomplished three things: first, it provided a scene of dramatic action for the hook; second, it provided part of the setting that I had neglected to include in the original version (descendants of a wrecked circus starship); third, and most important, the opening scene gives a dangerous, sinister quality to Yudo's presence in Fyx's home—something that was lacking in the original version.

SUMMARY

The opening of a story must hook the reader's attention and establish the story situation. The story situation is the character situation placed against the obstacle, establishing the main conflict.

Hooking the reader's attention may require searching along the story line to pick out a significantly dramatic moment (something is *happening*), moving that part of the story to the front, and backfilling the story situation before proceeding with the buildup.

In the same manner, either part of a buildup scene or climax scene may be moved to the front to form a hook. If a suitable hook cannot be found along the story line, or if removing part of a scene would disrupt the story's effect, a hook may be created by starting the story earlier (creating an action scene leading up to the story situation).

Within the story situation itself, at the moment the character meets its obstacle, the conflict inherent in such a situation may be all the hook that is needed, requiring nothing more than the proper structuring and treatment (through action) of the story situation.

Another method of creating a hook is to use a story frame, another story used as a setting for the main story. This can be done if the "frame story" opens in a compelling manner. In such cases, the main story within the frame serves as the frame story's buildup while the closing frame usually serves as a trailer to wind down the main story.

EXERCISES

1. What should the opening of a story contain?
2. Diagram the schematic of a complete story situation.
3. Write a complete story opening.
4. Diagram the schematics for four different kinds of "hooks."

5. Using the setting in "Untitled One," complete the story opening by supplying the missing parts.

6. Devise a complete story situation and write it in three different arrangements.

CHAPTER THREE

BACKFILL

The purpose of backfill is to explain to the reader the nature or existence of some event or thing that has taken place earlier in a story. For example, if you moved an action scene out of sequence to provide your story with a hook, the reasons why the characters are in that situation must be explained through backfill. Five main kinds of backfill are used: dream sequences, flashbacks, ignorant devices, parallel running scenes, and dialog or narrative references. There are two more kinds of backfill that should *not* be used: spear carriers and lectures.

You may combine any of the five kinds of backfill to produce further forms of backfill. For example, a dream sequence that is a flashback. The following examples contain different kinds of backfill. After each example are questions concerning the form of backfill used. Answer these questions before turning to the critiques at the end of the chapter.

DREAM SEQUENCE: A scene consisting of a viewpoint character's dream.

FLASHBACK: Bringing the reader to a scene chronologically prior to another scene.

IGNORANT DEVICE: Any passive device (recorders, transmitters, rocks, amulets, gods, etc.) that a character can talk to, conveying information that the author wishes to pass on to the reader.

PARALLEL RUNNING SCENES: A scene, or a separate story, that is broken up and interspersed among the scenes of the main story.

REFERENCE: Thinking, dialog among the characters, or narrative that provides information the author wishes to pass on to the reader.

LECTURE: Overly long dialog or narrative reference.

SPEAR CARRIER: A character dragged into a story for the sole purpose of having something the author wants the reader to know explained to him with no further character development; using characters as ignorant devices.

DREAM SEQUENCE/FLASHBACK
Example From **"Enemy Mine"**

The story situation consisted of two fighter pilots, one human, the other an alien, stranded on a tiny island on a planet plagued with high winds, tidal waves, freezing temperatures, and next to nothing to eat. The two pilots are enemies, but must at least call off the fight to work together and survive. Immediately preceding the dream sequence, the human (Davidge) has discovered that a large land mass exists far away, in the direction of the prevailing winds. The only thing that can float on the island is the alien pilot's ejection capsule. The alien (a Drac named Jeriba Shigan, called "Jerry" by Davidge) refuses to try the capsule in the water, and the scene following finds the two that night, in the stone shack they have built, still arguing about the capsule.

The winds pick up, causing larger waves than they had experienced before, making argument over the capsule academic. They seek safety in the capsule, and Davidge learns that Jerry (a hermaphrodite) is pregnant and had lost a child (*tean*) before in a fall, which is why the Drac didn't want to risk the voyage in the capsule. Waves crash about the capsule, smashing their stone shack. The story continues . . .

. . . So Jerry was afraid of losing another child. It was almost certain that the capsule trip would bang us around a lot, but staying on the sandbar didn't appear to be improving our chances. The capsule had been at rest for quite a while, and I decided to take a peek outside. The small canopy windows seemed to be covered with sand, and I opened the door. I looked around and all of the walls had been smashed flat. I looked toward the sea, but could see nothing. "It looks safe, Jerry. . ." I looked up, toward the blackish sky, and above me towered the white plume of a descending breaker. *"Maga* damn *sienna!"* I slammed the hatch door.

"*Ess,* Davidge?"

"Hang on, Jerry!"

The sound of the water hitting the capsule was beyond hearing. We banged once, twice against the rock, then we could feel ourselves twisting, shooting upward. I made a grab to hang on, but missed as the capsule took a sickening lurch downward. I fell into Jerry, then was flung to the opposite wall where I struck my head. Before I went blank, I heard Jerry cry *"Tean! Vi Tean!"*

. . . *the lieutenant pressed his hand control and a figure—tall, humanoid, yellow—appeared on the screen.*

"Dracslime!" shouted the auditorium of seated recruits.

The lieutenant faced the recruits. "Correct. This is a Drac. Note that the Drac race is uniform as to color; they are all yellow." The recruits chuckled politely. The officer preened a bit, then with a light-wand began pointing out various features. "The three-fingered hands are distinctive, of course, as is the almost noseless face, which gives the Drac a toad-like appearance. On average, eyesight is slightly better than human, hearing about the same, and smell . . ." The lieutenant paused. "The smell is terrible!" The officer beamed at the uproar from the recruits. When the auditorium quieted down, he pointed his light-wand at a fold in the figure's belly. "This is where the Drac keeps its family

jewels—all of them." Another chuckle. "That's right, Dracs are her-
maphrodites, with both male and female reproductive organs contained
in the same individual." The lieutenant faced the recruits. "You go tell
a Drac to go boff himself, then watch out, because he can!" The laughter
died down and the lieutenant held out a hand toward the screen. "You
see one of these things, what do you do?"
    "KILL IT . . . ."

    . . . I cleared the screen and computer sighted on the next Drac fighter,
looking like a double x in the screen's display. The Drac shifted hard
to the left, then right again. I felt the autopilot pull my ship after the
fighter, sorting out and ignoring the false images, trying to lock its
electronic crosshairs on the Drac. "Come on, toad face . . . a little bit to
the left . . ." The double cross image moved into the ranging rings on
my display and I felt the missile attached to the belly of my fighter take
off. "Gotcha!" Through my canopy I saw the flash as the missile deto-
nated. My screen showed the Drac fighter out of control, spinning toward
Fyrine IV's cloud-shrouded surface. I dived after it to confirm the
kill . . . skin temperature increasing as my ship brushed the upper at-
mosphere. "Come on, dammit, blow!" I shifted the ship's systems over
for atmospheric flight when it became obvious that I'd have to follow
the Drac right to the ground. Still above the clouds, the Drac stopped
spinning and turned. I hit the auto override and pulled the stick into
my lap. The fighter wallowed as it tried to pull up. Everyone knows the
Drac ships work better in atmosphere . . . heading toward me on an
interception course . . . why doesn't the slime fire? . . . just before the
collision, the Drac ejects . . . power gone; have to deadstick it in. I track
the capsule as it falls through the muck, intending to find that Dracslime
and finish the job . . .

    It could have been for seconds or years that I groped into the darkness
around me. I felt touching, but the parts of me being touched seemed
far, far away. First chills, then fever, then chills again, my head being
cooled by a gentle hand. I opened my eyes to narrow slits and saw
Jerry hovering over me, blotting my forehead with something cool. I
managed a whisper. "Jerry."
    The Drac looked into my eyes and smiled. "Good is, Davidge. Good
is."
    The light on Jerry's face flickered and I smelled smoke. "Fire."
    Jerry got out of the way and pointed to the room's sandy floor. I let
my head roll over and realized that I was lying on a bed of springy
branches. Opposite my bed was another bed, and between them crack-
led a cheery campfire. "Fire we now have, Davidge. And wood." Jerry
pointed toward the roof made of wooden poles thatched with broad
leaves.
    I turned and looked around, then let my throbbing head sink down
and closed my eyes. "Where are we?"
    "Big island, Davidge. Soaker off sandbar us washed. Wind and waves

us here took. Right you were."

"I . . . I don't understand; *ne gavey*. It'd take days to get to the big island from the sandbar."

Jerry nodded and dropped what looked like a sponge into a shell of some sort filled with water. "Nine days. You I strap to *nasesay*, then on beach here we land."

"Nine days? I've been out for nine days?"

Jerry shook its head. "Seventeen. Here we land eight days . . ." The Drac waved its hand behind itself.

"Ago . . . eight days ago."

"*Ae.*"

Dream Sequence/Flashback: **"Enemy Mine"**

The story began at the point where Davidge and Jeriba Shigan first met on the island face-to-face, fighting it out barehanded. Instead of using the second dream sequence, I could have begun the story earlier with the dogfight in space. Instead of using the first dream sequence, I could have begun the story even earlier, with Davidge's recruit training. If I had begun there, I could have eliminated both sequences.

1. What did I accomplish by starting the story on the island?
2. What did I accomplish by inserting the dream sequences where I did?
3. Immediately following the dream sequences, another form of backfill is used; what is it?

DREAM SEQUENCE

Example From **"The Homecoming"**

Baxter tossed on his pallet, his fingers clawing at his mind's monsters. *He saw himself, a fraud in man's clothing. A creature of petty evasion, weak, frightened—above all, frightened. Thin hands reached out to work levers and turn knobs; watery eyes, reflective and darting, sought out lights and dials. Shaking and pain-whipped, the creature operated a machine. Baxter's view faded back, through the wall of the machine, into the light. He stumbled as his view of the machine reached a point of recognition. With thick painted lips, gleaming cardboard teeth, and dime store flashlight bulbs for eyes, Carl Baxter raised a hand in his direction . . . the machine-Baxter buzzed as the creature inside screamed. . . .*

Dream Sequence: **"The Homecoming"**

The dream sequence above is nothing more than Carl Baxter's nightmare; it does not depict either the story past, present, or future.

1. What information does it convey to the reader?

Example From **"The Homecoming"**
Lothas draped his heavy green tail between the seat cushion and backrest. Extending a claw on a scaled, five-fingered hand, he inserted it in a slotswitch and pulled down. The armored shield on the forward view bubble slowly lifted as the control center went to redlight. Lothas felt the strange pain grow in his chest as he looked through the filter at the target star, now no longer a point of light but a tiny, brilliant disc. He leaned against the backrest, his large dark eyes glittering as they drank in the sight of the star. *It has been so long. Even though I have been out of suspension for only a total of six star cycles, yet I know it has been . . . seventy million star cycles. A third of a galactic cycle.*

Lothas noticed his own reflection in the filter, turned his long neck left, then right, and marveled at the absence of change. The large eyes, occupying a fifth of the image, were clear and glinted with points of red, blue and yellow light reflected from service and indicator lights. The skin, gray-green and smooth, pressed against and outlined the large veins leading from his eyes down the elongated muzzle with its rows of thick, white, needle-sharp teeth. His focus returned to the star as he reached and pressed a panel with one of the five clawed fingers of his right hand.

"This is Lothas Dim Ir, on regular watch." He paused and examined the navigation readout, then switched to a display of the rest of the cluster formation of ships. "The formation is normal; no course corrections necessary; the homestar Amasaat now at . . ." he examined an instrument, ". . . four degrees of arc."

He pressed another panel, signaling to all the watches on the rest of the ships. The display showed all but three of the two hundred ships answering. Lothas studied the display, slightly confused that he felt nothing about the missing ships. Automatic recording systems had shown the three ships wrecked by the same meteor. *But that was . . . millions of cycles ago. Difficult to feel pain for deaths that old.*

He pressed another panel, and the display began filling with life-unit survival-percentage figures transmitted by the watches on the other ships. Automatically an average and a total rate of survival and unit count was made. 77.031%; 308,124 life-units surviving. Lothas nodded. There had been no change in the figure for . . . over thirty million star cycles. The three wrecked ships, and the others who could not survive the suspension process. *But, the rest of us shall see Nitola.*

Ignorant Devices & Reference: **"The Homecoming"**
The same information could have been conveyed to the reader by having two or more of the critters conversing.

1. Even if done briefly, avoiding lectures, what is the main story problem caused by using dialog between the characters to establish this story situation?
2. What effect was created by limiting the opening scene to one character?

FLASHBACK

Example From **"The Jaren"**

. . . Eeola sat on a rocky outcropping overlooking a steep cliff. The jungle floor spread out into the distance, and on the horizon stood the peculiar landmark that marked the center of my property. In the bright light of Adn, Baalphor's only moon, the feature seemed larger than I remembered seeing it during the day. It was a portion of the jungle floor, risen on a huge cake-shaped formation of rock. I turned from it to see the old Shikki finishing off his bottle of Purim.

"My friends didn't mean to hurt your feelings. Come back to the fire."

Eeola issued one sharp laugh, then tossed his empty bottle over the cliff. He laughed again, then listened as the bottle smashed on the rocks below. "They do not hurt my feelings." He shook his head. "I should have said nothing, but this place," he held his hands out toward the landmark, "it loosens a drunken tongue."

I lowered myself and sat on a rock facing the Shikki. "This place has special meaning to you?"

Eeola shook his head. "It is of no interest to you."

I held out my hands. "Then why did I ask?"

The Shikki shrugged. "To understand the meaning of this place to me, you must understand me, and for that . . ." he held up an arm and pointed at the sky, ". . . you must understand from where I came." He dropped the arm into his lap and shook his head. "Too much understanding from a human."

I was not used to Shikkies talking to me in that manner, and my face grew hot. But for some reason I held my peace. Eeola sat quietly, and for such a long time, I felt certain the old fellow had passed out. I was about to leave when a pale blue shimmering began in the jungle below. It faded, then began again in a new place. It faded once again and I strained my eyes for it. I turned to Eeola to ask him about it, and the blue light passed between me and the Shikki, then seemed to settle beside him. I could not move; it was as though my buttocks had become rooted to the rock. After a few moments, another such light joined the first, then another, and another, until four separate lights made a circle, with Eeola forming a fifth part of it. Slowly Eeola turned his head, until he faced me.

"Then, listen, human, while I take words and grant life to those who I am not yet able to grant death."

I would tell you of my Jaren; of Vastar, our warrior *Di*, who took the charge in battle much as he did when we were children; of Gemislor, whose broad back and jokes held us together through flame and privation; of mighty Dob, whose ruthlessness on the field of battle was matched only by his gentleness with a lost or hungry animal; of Timbenevva, whose pipes could make flagging spirits soar, and whose sly tongue could talk the very stars from the sky; and of myself. I, Eeola, was the youngest member of the Jaren.

. . . Before entering the military, before adulthood, before instruction at the village *kiruch,* as naked children playing at war with moss forts and water guns, the Jaren is formed. Over forty Earth years ago, in my village on the planet Tenuet, my story begins. . . .

Flashback: **"The Jaren"**

The main problem with flashbacks is that they require picking up the reader and hustling him to a prior point in story time. In other words, the story is going backwards, not forwards. However, there is often no other way to tell a particular story. Once the reader has been taken back into the past, there is no problem. The story is again going forward. But the reader must be willing to be brought back in time, which means that the transition between the present and the past must be carefully done.

1. The transition in "The Jaren" worked for three reasons. What are they?

PARALLEL RUNNING SCENES

Example From **"Project Fear"**

As was explained in Chapter Two, to provide an effective hook for this story it was necessary to split the climax scene, moving part of it to the front. A further rewrite was requested because more character development was needed. The hook I used also introduced the character of Miklynn, which inspired me to expand the climax scene, split it up and spread it throughout the story, using those segments to provide needed characterization. This was made possible because "the thing's" defense mechanism was to bring one's deepest fears literally to the surface—in such a manner that those fears became visible to everyone else. Such scenes as the following were placed in parallel with the main story (the scene takes place outside the Academy administration building after the confrontation between Miklynn and Lua. Dean has just been introduced to Parks, a member of Miklynn's team):

. . . Miklynn turned toward me. "Now I want the answer to my question."

I frowned. "What question?"

"You a garry or a Christer?"

I felt my face grow hot. "I don't think that's any of your business!"

Miklynn stabbed a forefinger in my chest. "It's my business, schoolboy. Now answer the question or take a hike."

"Miklynn, I'll go or stay as I damn well please!"

He studied me with his tiny eyes. "Hit the bricks, schoolboy. I don't need you."

I thrust out my chin. "You don't own this place. If I feel like going, I'll go. Right now I don't feel like it."

Miklynn stabbed his finger in my chest again. "Get going, schoolboy, before I get mean."

"Hell no, you tub of guts!" Perhaps insanity runs in my family. Nevertheless, I hauled off and drove my fist into Miklynn's big belly. It sank in six centimeters, then met a hard wall of muscle. I don't even think Miklynn blinked. Then, just swinging his fist from where his arm was at his side, he drove it into my stomach. When my head cleared, I was flat on my back, clutching my middle.

Miklynn looked at Parks. "I finally tracked down Arango. I have to go get him."

"Where was he? In jail?"

"Where else?" Miklynn turned to leave.

Parks pointed a finger at me. "What about this one?"

Miklynn stopped, looked at me, then rubbed his chin. He turned and talked over his shoulder as he left. "Sign him up, Parks. We can always use a clown with a death wish."

I see it—I see his . . . his fear. Miklynn has fear, too. A young child, poor, father unemployed, mother drinking, brother in prison—failures all. Failure. He takes them on in the reformatory; boys older, stronger, and whips them. Always a larger, more difficult challenge, to prove something—that he is no failure, and he always wins. He never fails, yet the fear is failure. Does he see his own soul the way I see it? Tears stream down Miklynn's face, he holds out his hands. "Oh, stop it! Stop it!"

I pull my glance away, cowering from the flames, then Parks—his living soul spread on the ground. A life of God, ordination, a Corps chaplain—then he rejects it all. The guilt. Have mercy, the guilt! He believes this . . . this is his due. His proper punishment. His fear—that he was wrong. I feel the hot breath of the sky on my face. "Parks! Parks!"

That afternoon, soon after I had completed my outprocessing and had been issued my diploma, Parks and I sat on a pile of equipment at the Ninth Quadrant Base adjoining the Academy complex. . . .

Parallel Running Scenes: **"Project Fear"**

1. Parallel running scenes have several advantages over other kinds of backfill. What are they?
2. What is this form of backfill's one big disadvantage?

LECTURES

Example From **"SHAWNA, Ltd."**

The example below begins at the point where Rawls, a semanticist charged with "souping up" SHAWNA flight, is asking questions of Captain Sanford, head of SHAWNA Ltd.'s philosophical flight school.

"Perhaps you could explain a bit about how SHAWNA works."

"Of course. First, external objects depend upon mind for existence. This has been known for centuries—the so-called miraculous cures without the aid of medicine, a life completely changed because one believed strongly enough, 'faith can move mountains,' and so on. Even your own discipline provided a thread of the evidence with Alfred Korzybski's theory of the self-fulfilling prophecy: you think disaster will happen, and because of the thought, disaster happens. Am I clear thus far?"

"Yes, I think so."

Sanford cleared his throat. "Well, the inventors of SHAWNA twenty-six years ago discovered the component of mind that contains this power to create and shape reality, and they discovered how to amplify it. Thus, a mind amplified by SHAWNA can, in effect, think itself wherever it wants to go. All that need be done is to proceed on a firm philosophical foundation, dissolve the reality around you, then construct the reality you desire. With the trip we are about to take, for example, the reality of Earth will be dissolved around the ship, and the reality of the planet Betelvane will be created."

Rawls nibbled at his lower lip. "I know flights such as this have been going on for years, but . . . when the reality of Earth is dissolved . . . what happens to those on Earth?"

Sanford chuckled. "Remember, Doctor, there are many minds involved here, each one establishing the substance of its own reality. Those on Earth see themselves here, and see the reality of Earth; therefore, for them, nothing changes. But the amplified perceptions of the philosopher pilots override the perceptions of others about the ship's location. The amplified mind dissolves and creates reality for those aboard the ship. Thus, almost instant travel across light-year distances. . . ."

Lectures: **"SHAWNA, Ltd."**

A lecture is an expanded form of backfill by reference, and the lectures in the original version of "SHAWNA, Ltd." are classic.

1. What are the two main story problems caused by using lectures?
2. There is a third problem caused by using this particular lecture within this particular story situation; what is it?

CRITIQUES

Dream Sequence: **"Enemy Mine"**

The main conflict and story situation in this story involve two enemies against the planet upon which they are stranded. By beginning the story where I did, the story situation was established within the first few lines. If I had started with the dogfight, I would have had to develop the space war scene—making it even longer—which would have taken me that much more verbiage to establish the story situation. In addition, since it isn't a space war story, beginning with the dogfight would have been a false signal to the reader. Those looking for a war in space story would have been disappointed and those bored with space wars never would have made it past the first scene. For the same reasons, I did not begin the story with Davidge's recruit training. Beginning the story on the island, however, requires some backfilling to add depth to the situation. But why use dream sequences, and why did I insert them where I did?

The double dream sequence in "Enemy Mine" was intended to accomplish three things: First, before the tidal waves struck, the two enemies were getting almost chummy; the reader needed a reminder as to how far these two characters had evolved in their relationship. Second, the second part of the dream sequence backfilled how the two characters found themselves stranded on the island, while both dream sequences highlighted the degree of racial hate that motivated at least the character of Davidge. Third, and most important, the double dream sequence saved me from having to take the reader through the seventeen days it took to get from the sandbar to the larger land mass and bring Davidge back to health. The days on Fyrine IV are twice as long as Earth Days, and I was already juggling a 35,000 word story intended for a magazine.

Another form of backfill was used immediately after the dream sequences: reference. In the conversation after the dream sequence where Jerry is explaining to Davidge what has happened, Jerry is "referring" to the events that led to the current situation, backfilling the previous seventeen days.

Fig. 3/1, Dream Sequence/Flashback

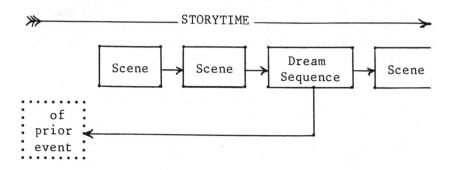

Dream Sequence: **"The Homecoming"**

The dream sequence in "The Homecoming" was used to provide characterization. In particular, it was used to show how the character of Carl Baxter saw himself. This is important to the story because Baxter has been virtually charged with the salvation of the human race through chance circumstance, and he finds himself totally inept to rise to the task. Before the dream sequence, he *feels* this; after the sequence, he *knows*.

Ignorant Devices & References: **"The Homecoming"**

George H. Scithers wanted a story about intelligent dinosaurs—inhabitants

Fig. 3/2, Dream Sequence

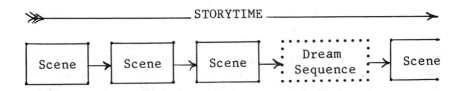

of Earth from seventy million years ago who show up in the present for fun and games. I selected ships with the dinosaurs traveling in suspended animation as the vehicle. In the opening scene I had to establish the story situation and at least partially backfill the past seventy million years; and all this while trying to create two effects: the aloneness of those who have stood the watches during that seventy-million-year-long voyage, and their longing to return to their home planet. Using dialog between two or more of the critters would have been less effective than one character alone in creating these two effects.

The main story problem with conveying this information to the reader through dialog, however, is that *all* of the critters already *know* all of the information. The content of the conversation, therefore, would be characters telling each other stuff that everybody (in the story) already knows. Whatever you think of dinosaurs, this is not plausible behavior.

To establish the effect—the meaning of the opening scene and situation to the creature—it had to be alone, reflecting on the vastness of the voyage almost concluded, and the goal almost attained. In this novella I used narrative reference, thinking reference, observation, description, and the ignorant devices of the ship's voice log and instruments. All of these can be used for backfill without requiring the presence of another character in the scene.

A caution: Do not use story characters as "ignorant devices." Do not, in other words, create a character simply to have him wander into a scene to have something explained to him for the reader's benefit. These creatures are called "spear carriers," and a story burdened with them will not convince. Story characters need to be developed to be convincing, and unless you can spare the words to develop a character and work him into the story, use another means of backfill.

"The Homecoming" was a prime candidate for a backfill problem that makes frequent appearances in stories: backfilling too much. To set up the story situation and put those lizards on those ships, I had to do research on several types of dinosaurs, what "man" was seventy million years ago, what Earth was like then, and I had to create the history of this particular kind of dinosaur and the reasons why it took to the sky. For each page of story, there was another page of research notes—good stuff, too. It is a temptation, after collecting all of that information, to inflict it upon the reader. Don't. Save it for a nonfiction article, but don't burden the story with any more than is necessary for the telling.

Flashbacks: **"The Jaren"**

The flashback in "The Jaren" was done as part of the story present. The entire main story is one long flashback, but because a character is telling you the flashback part within the context of the "frame story," the flashback doesn't appear to be a trip into the past. Instead, we are sitting next to the narrator, in story time present, listening to Eeola tell his story. This moves the reader into the story past without jarring him.

The second reason why the transition worked is because the story present leading into the flashback is *not* a compelling action scene. The worst thing you can do is to have a character up to his eyeballs in alligators, then continue with: "But first, let me tell you how this came to be. Years ago . . ." The reader will overshoot such an attempt at being yanked into the past: he wants to know what's going to happen next to the guy in the alligator pit! In "The Jaren," two beings are sitting upon rocks talking.

The third reason the transition worked is because plants were put into the opening scene that indicated to the reader that the story to be told by Eeola would be more interesting than the story present. Eeola obviously is suffering deep pain, the location of the scene is somehow connected with that pain, he comes from another world, belongs to a defeated warrior-race yet claims not to have been conquered, and four ghostly apparitions sit down next to us (the narrator) to listen to the story in which all will be made clear. *Indeed* we are curious to know what that story is.

In "Priest of the *Baraboo*," a similar device was used, in that the flashback was a chapter of a book read out loud by a character within the "frame story." In my novel, *City of Baraboo,* the extended flashback was a document within a "frame document," within a "frame story." In all three cases, the flashbacks appeared as part of the story present, rather than as trips to the past. In all three cases, the transition is *not* inserted at a point in the story containing compelling action. In all three cases, plants in the story present were used to intrigue the reader into exploring the story past.

Parallel Running Scenes: **"Project Fear"**
Because of the number of characters, and the low-keyed nature of the plot in this story, dumping usual characterization all over the place (through dialog, for example) would have made for tiresome reading. But because of the unusual way Dean gets the character information from "the thing," it's not tiresome at all. In fact, since in those scenes Dean is virtually hysterical with terror, the actual information could be highly abbreviated—keeping down the word count.

Parallel running scenes avoid the risk of taking the reader on a tour of the past, since the scene or story running parallel to the main story is either being observed, thought, remembered, or experienced in story time present. In fact, since the scene being run parallel to the main story was the climax scene, the reader was actually being given glimpses into the future, although the reader is never sure which set of scenes is either past, present or future until the end of the story. An additional benefit to using parallel running scenes in this story was in establishing and maintaining suspense through the low-keyed buildup, actually heightening the contrast between what the planet appeared to be and what it was.

Parallel running scenes are common in novel-length works ("Meanwhile, back at the ranch . . ."), but less so in short stories. This is because the structures of

Fig. 3/3, Parallel Running Scenes

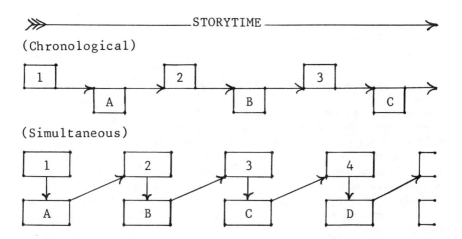

shorter works are not always adaptable to this form. You can easily give away endings, make certain kinds of effects impossible to achieve, or make clean, understandable plots hopelessly confused.

Lectures: **"SHAWNA, Ltd."**

The first story problem caused by a lecture is reader resentment. No one likes to be lectured, and there are few readers slow enough not to realize that, even though the characters are lecturing each other, it is the author who is lecturing the reader. The second story problem caused by a lecture is reader boredom. As with solid blocks of description, during stretches of lecturing, the story is spinning its wheels; the story is not *moving*. I can't think of a single instance where lecturing can be considered an effective form of backfill; but it is especially deadly in humor.

Backfilling through dialog reference can easily turn into lectures unless you ask yourself: "Is anything happening in this scene besides two or more characters flapping their gums?" If the answer is no, either make the scene *very* short, eliminate it, or use another form of backfill.

The third problem, peculiar to this particular lecture, is that it is not plausible that Rawls would know *nothing* about the workings of the biggest technological achievement known to his generation—especially since it is related to his own field.

SUMMARY

The purpose of backfill is to explain the existence or nature of a prior situation or event. Backfill can be used to back up a hook with a piece's story situation, or it can be used anywhere along the story line where explanation is needed to establish a current situation. Spear carriers and lectures should be avoided. The first is not convincing and the second is boring. No amount of skill can make up for the faults inherent in these two methods. Flashbacks must be approached with care. If at all possible, make them parts of the current story line, rather than taking the reader on a trip into the past. In using other forms of backfill, never have one character explaining to the second character that which the second character already knows.

EXERCISES

Story Situation: **"Forward Private Aaldz"**

Setting: equatorial belt of the planet Jadduk in the year (Earth time) 2217. Jadduk is the second planet orbiting a G star (yellow), with .78 Earth Gravity, oxygen-nitrogen atmosphere, sparse vegetation except at the planet's poles where the native population lives under tropical rain forest conditions. Jadduk's equatorial region is a hot, dusty desert. The equatorial belt of Jadduk has been occupied as a training facility by Tourlemaine Guard: one of the several armies of a wide-reaching, wealthy, powerful empire. The soldiers in the Guard are entirely human.

Character: Aaldz ne Cru-dim, a native of Jadduk. The Jadduks are a primitive race of intelligent swamp dwellers, with physiologies resembling that of salamanders. They can stand upright, standing approximately 1.45 meters tall when adult. For a long time Aaldz has watched Guard training exercises, marveling at the glitter and excitement of what he perceives as life in the Guard as compared to his dreary swamp existence. Through contacts with the various and sundry beings that act as a support and supply force for the Guard, Aaldz learns the basics of the human language, bids his friends and relatives good-bye, and strikes out for the equatorial belt. Aaldz wants to join the Guard.

Obstacle: The humans do not take the Jadduks seriously, the Guard is made up of humans, and no one has any intention of having that state of affairs change. Diversions for the soldiers on Jadduk are few, however. They find the eager Aaldz amusing and decide to enter him in "special" recruit training—designed to put the innocent swamp dweller through a series of cruel, impossible, unbearable tasks.

Main Conflict: During one of the "tasks," Aaldz realizes that he is not being taken seriously by the soldiers; that he is only being made fun of and that the soldiers have no intention of letting him enter the Guard.

Problem: Aaldz wants to enter the Guard; he decides that he *will* be taken seriously.

Using the action of one of the "tasks" for a hook, complete the opening of "Forward Private Aaldz" by backfilling the complete story situation (supplying the information above). Backfill your hook through:

1. A dream sequence.
2. A flashback.
3. The use of ignorant devices.
4. The use of reference.

5. Parallel running scenes.
6. A combination of two or more types of backfill.

CHAPTER FOUR

OTHER PARTS

TITLES

A title should not be tacked onto your story as an afterthought nor otherwise regarded as of little importance. This is for the same reason that Joy is not called "Cheap Dish Soap." A title is the name or label which identifies your story and to a degree introduces it to the reader. Your story won't be rejected because of a bad title, but by the same token, your story might get published *with* a bad title. Coming up with the right title is *your* job.

In most cases the title for your story should be drawn from either the story's main theme or core idea. To do this, it is necessary to identify those elements of your story. A clear statement of your theme will hand you your title in the majority of cases. Below are statements of story themes and ideas of mine, the titles that came from them, and how they were derived:

The idea was a society where news is conveyed by "newstellers" who must present the news in the form of structured stories. In this society, news is considered more a form of entertainment than a means of getting information. Because newstelling is performing, newstelling "acts" must be taken on the road, tried out, rewritten, and polished before being taken in front of large city audiences, much like plays open first in New Haven and Philadelphia before being taken to Broadway. The story depicts one of these performances, which handed me the obvious title: "The Tryouts."

Two enemies are stranded on a hostile planet and must work together to survive. A principal subplot of the story was one of the characters being his own worst enemy. I had just gotten the general story situation clear in my mind, and was watching David Niven in *The Best of Enemies* on television, when the title popped into my head: "Enemy Mine." Why not "My Enemy," or "The Enemies"? I not only liked the sound of "Enemy Mine," but the construction resembled the English/Drac pidgin language the two characters used while they were learning each other's tongue.

Intelligent dinosaurs leave Earth seventy million years ago and return in the present to reclaim their planet. The human who must treat with these creatures is a weak sort who is torn from the comfort of his routine and is thrown in among these dinosaurs to deal for the survival of both his home and that of humanity's. What else to call this tale but "Homecoming"?

However, there were titles that were harder to come by. One story involved an old circus rider's efforts to keep alive his art in the face of impossible odds. Performing horses require the existence of a circus, but no circus existed on the planet Momus. The old man owns four performing "liberty" horses, but his four sons all had left to work at driving timber nags. But what to use for a title? After everything else had failed, I turned to *Bartlett's Quotations* and looked up everything containing the word "horse." After much searching, I found the following:

> Round-hoof'd, short-jointed, fetlocks shag and long,
> Broad breast, full eye, small head and nostril wide,
> High crest, short ears, straight legs and passing strong,
> Thin mane, thick tail, broad buttock, tender hide:
> Look, what a horse should have he did not lack,
> Save a proud rider on so proud a back.
> —Shakespeare, *Venus and Adonis*

The title for the story became "Proud Rider." In fact, the quote was such a perfect statement of the story's theme, I ran it before the story.

Another tough title involved an old Moman storyteller who set out on a peculiar kind of adventure to restoke his fiction fires. The story situation was not firm in my mind, but that it was going to be humorous had already been decided. I like to begin a story with the title already in place because it helps to guide the story's direction. Still, a suitable title eluded me until it occurred to me that there were some striking character similarities between Pulsit the storyteller and that famous knight Don Quixote. I went to Boston to see the play *Man of La Mancha* and left with the title: "The Quest."

One method of inventing a title that rarely fails is to "force" a title. With your story completed, begin making a list of titles, one right after another, as fast as you can—no matter how silly or trite—until you have ten or twenty titles. If you are fortunate, one of them will leap out at you as the exact fit for your story. If none of them seem good, put the list away and go to bed. What your effort will have done is to gear your subconscious mind to the task of coming up with the right title. While you sleep, your head will be working on the problem. When you wake up, in the majority of cases, the right title will be sitting on your nose.

Many times you will come up with a title that has no story. Take notes on these and file them away. Every now and then one of those titles will grow into a full-blown story; at other times you will have written a story and can't find a title for it. This happened to Stanley Schmidt. Then, in the bathtub, he recalled a title he had filed away years before: "A Flash of Darkness." They matched.

BUILDUPS

The total of the events in a story that transpire between the introduction of the problem and the story's climax is called the buildup. There are different kinds of buildups used according to the kind of story you are doing. An important aspect of all buildups is pacing. Pacing is the rate of words per event in the story. Rapid pacing is few words per event; slow or low-keyed pacing has a higher number of words per event—the story moves more slowly.

SAGA. The saga buildup, of whatever length, is a simple chronological relating of the events of the story. The character is faced with a problem, we follow the events of his life over the course of minutes, hours, days, or years, until he resolves his problem. The effect of the saga buildup does not necessitate rapid scene pacing, warted horrors behind every tree, nor a sword-swinging climax. Instead, the problem may be in the character's mind, the events we follow affect his mind, and the problem's resolution may transpire there. The pacing in sagas may be very low-keyed, such as in "boy becomes man" or "a day in the life of" pieces. Such pieces can use ordinary "backyard" settings, since the problem, its importance to the character, and the problem's resolution are the most important features of the story.

ADVENTURE. Structurally the adventure story is similar to the saga. The character has a goal and the reader follows the character in his attempts to achieve his goal. The main differences are that unusual, dangerous settings, and frequent moments of intense action building to an action-packed climax both reflect the character's problem, and often are more important to the story than the problem. The pacing of the adventure story—moving the character from one action-packed challenge to the next—is very important to maintain reader interest. As was mentioned before, avoid repeating the same scene structure over and over again. Repeated scene structures can take the most heroic efforts and reduce them to monotony.

ESCAPE. The escape story is much like an adventure story limited in that the character's main goal is to get free from whatever his obstacle is: jailer, system, society, creatures, mental devils, or whatever. Again, avoid repeating scene structures.

HORROR/TERROR. Both horror and terror stories rest on scaring the reader to fulfill their purposes, and both use danger to the character(s) as the vehicle. Varied pacing—very slow, followed by rapid—can be used to great effect: character sitting alone in a room waiting, waiting, waiting . . . *then "It" springs at him!* (going "boo!" at the reader). As with the adventure story, the form of the problem is sometimes more significant to the success of the story than is the problem.

I find it helps me to distinguish between horror and terror stories in the following manner: terror stories throw the character into an environment of fear caused by all-too-believable, ordinary persons or events in commonplace settings. For example, in my story "A Time For Terror," published in *IA'sfm* under the name Frederick Longbeard, a character is captured on Luna by a brutal band of terrorists who are hatching a plot to infect Earth with a hideous product of recombinant DNA engineering. Nothing about this story—terrorists, the setting, biological blackmail—is out of the ordinary. Realizing that in the very near future this fiction could be fact is one of the things that makes the story scary.

Horror stories depend, instead, on things bordering more on the weird and wonderful. For example, in "Project Fear" the thing being confronted was a single lifeform that almost covered the surface of a planet, whose first line of defense was to bring one's fears to a conscious, visible, tactile level. In the horror story, making the "thing" both horrible and believable is what makes it scary.

MYSTERY. The mystery story requires that a crime be committed and at least one character's goal is to find out who did it. Next the character must be presented with a number of possible wrongdoers. Throughout the buildup—however paced—three kinds of clues must be presented to both sleuth and reader. The first kind of clue is evidence pointing to the guilty party. The second kind of clue is evidence pointing to the innocent suspects. The third kind of clue is evidence canceling out the second kind of clue such that if a computer processed all of the clues, the guilty party's name would pop out of the answer slot.

To play this game successfully, you must present your false accusatory clues very clearly, your clues pointing to the real criminal with somewhat less clarity, and your evidence clearing the innocent almost as parts of the incidental background ("Surely, Watson, you must have noticed the tarnished left tine on the pickle fork?"). Usually, to give the reader a fighting chance at discovering the real culprit before your sleuth, mystery buildups are rather low-keyed, leaving the clue-gathering and puzzle-solving processes the main events.

PUZZLE. The puzzle story is a type of mystery; but instead of the reader trying to find out whodunit, the reader must try to figure out what is going on. Again, you must supply the reader with enough information to figure it out before the story's punchline, and enough additional information to make the reader rush off to the wrong conclusion. If you don't supply the puzzle-solving clues, the story is not a puzzle story; it is a "tomato surprise." If you've made it too easy for the reader, the story then becomes "predictable."

BUILDUP COMBINATIONS. All of the buildups above can be combined to produce story variations. For example, through an evolution of rewrites, "Project Fear" moved from being a saga to a saga/horror story. "The Magician's Apprentice," on the other hand, was a saga/puzzle story. All buildup forms and combinations are subject, as well, to being either serious, humorous, or both.

BRIGHT & DARK MOMENTS

Bright and dark moments are used in the story's buildup to do two principal things: (1) to make plot twists and the ending of the story unpredictable; and, (2) to wreak havoc on the reader's emotions.

Bright moments can be anything from feeding your character a slim straw of hope to convincing him that all of the obstacles between him and his goal have been overcome. To a reader who has identified with your character, the bright moment comes as an exultant lift. Because of formula writing in both literature and visual media, the reader then expects to get slammed with a Dark Moment: it all falls apart. Be unpredictable. Run two bright moments in a row, or run nothing but dark moments until the final victory. The dark moment near the end is a signal to the reader for a happy ending. Follow that with a dark moment and be unpredictable. A bright moment toward the end signals an unhappy ending; give the reader a convincing happy ending and be just as unpredictable.

There are several kinds of compliments handed to writers. Among them I value only one thing higher than laughter: tears. You have to dig more deeply into a reader's gut to extract tears, which is why they have more value. Create an admirable character, have the reader fall in love with him, then kill him.

Create an abominable character, cause the reader to hate him, then cause the character to change, altering the reader's perception and emotional reaction to the character. It has been said many times that the big thrill of being a writer is playing God. I have no quibble with this, except that many writers perceive this only as an ability to move characters around on paper. It is a poor sort of god that can only direct fictional characters. I look at it differently; by moving the characters, I move readers.

This might all sound very calculated (here I shall cause a laugh; there a tear). This is not the case, at least with me. When I am writing a story, bright and dark moments are dictated by what I "feel" the story needs at any given point. I do not make a conscious effort to tweak the reader into a chuckle or a tear; what I put in is put in only because it seems "right" at the time. It is very subjective. But even so, it is founded upon my awareness of what bright and dark moments will do within a given story situation. During rewriting, however, because I can take a more objective view of the story, I can afford to become more calculating. Bright moments can be polished, making them brighter; dark moments can be painted even blacker; either can be exchanged, inserted, or deleted according to my perception of how the alteration will affect both the story and the reader.

PLANTS

In science fiction and fantasy, as well as in a good deal of mainstream fiction, the author is frequently faced with preparing the reader to accept an improbable story situation or turn of events. Plants are props, comments, and items of information placed prior to the improbable event to prepare the reader to accept the event or situation. A character cannot simply step into a time machine and zip off to the future; plants must have been placed to signal to the reader that time travel is not only possible, but is a fact. You can't have a vampire munching on his most recent victim beginning with line one; you have to lay plants for the reader to cause him to suspect that vampires exist—then on with the munching.

Often a few indications will be sufficient: hubby's boss doesn't reflect an image in the mirror; he appears to have an aversion to the garlic bread you've prepared, and so on. Another way is called "sucking in the reader." This is a symphony of plants that begins by presenting a totally believable situation, then replacing it in swallowable bites until the reader has eaten the whole thing.

If Joe is to get his brains blown out, the gun must exist prior to the event. If Mary is to get gnawed by Count Dracula, the existence of vampires must be established before the event. If a character makes an unpredictable decision, altering the course of the story, the qualities of the character that fathered that decision must be established prior to the event. By whatever device, these preparations are called "plants." Caution: do *not* enter plants that are not to be used. If there is a gun on the table, someone later on better pick it up and shoot it. Plants that are not used tend to trouble the reader's mind after the story is finished. Why *was* that gun on the table? What purpose did it serve? Things in stories that cause such questions leave the reader unsatisfied and are called "loose ends."

Everything within your story will be pointing toward the story's conflict and the ultimate resolution of that conflict. Do not telegraph the ending of your story. The reader who guesses your ending before you unfold it will feel cheated. Avoid this by not adhering to hoary formulas. Also let yourself surprise yourself. Upon approaching the end of a story, you will find a pause in which you will be asking yourself: "What would the reader expect?" "What do *I* want?" "What is *right* for the story?" Every story has a number of endings; once you boil down all of those questions, the "right" ending will present itself—whether you like that particular ending or not.

ENDINGS

The ending of your story must resolve the story's main conflict; it must resolve any remaining secondary conflicts, questions, or issues (loose ends); and it must satisfy the reader. To do this, your ending, first, must be the believable consequence of the events that transpired within the tale. If it is not believable, it will not convince. Second, the ending must be unexpected. Predictable endings leave the reader feeling cheated. Third, the ending must not be cheap or easy ("Then I woke up—and it was all a dream!"). Cheap endings leave the reader feeling highly unsatisfied. In setting up a story situation, you have created an equation of circumstances. There is a "right" answer to such an equation, but each story situation can have more than one "right" answer.

To resolve the main conflict, either your character overcomes the obstacle or is defeated in his attempts to overcome it. Secondary conflicts are resolved in the same manner. Questions and issues raised during the story must either be decided, or removed by rewriting them from the body of the story. Believability is achieved by your ending being consistent with the premises and universe of your story, being consistent with understandable motivation and behavior, and through the use of properly laid plants. Just as a reader needs to be prepared to accept an unusual premise at the beginning of a story, preparation is needed to accept a startling ending.

In many cases an ending will be unpredictable simply because the reader has no idea how the story will resolve. The twist ending is a different case. To do a twist ending, you purposefully lay plants throughout the story pointing toward a particular ending, thereby leading the reader to expect that ending. Then the ending is completely different than the one expected by the reader. To make such an ending believable, you must do two things: first, all of the plants pointing toward the expected ending must be explainable in terms of the twist ending; second, disguised plants must be laid throughout the story pointing toward the twist ending—preparing the reader for it.

TRAILERS

A trailer is a special kind of ending that consists of a brief scene following the story's climax scene. In shorter works, the climax scene should contain everything needed to conclude the story; but in longer works chopping off the story at the end of the climax scene might be too abrupt. The trailer allows you to wind down the story a bit, as well as to give the reader an additional kick, insight, or chuckle. Below are the descriptions and purposes of a few trailers used in several of my stories.

In **"Homecoming"** the trailer consisted of a scene with two of the dinosaurs on the bridge of their lead ship. The ship is heading away from Earth and the two characters are reflecting on their experience with the humans. The scene accomplished two things: it showed what those creatures would be doing after the end of the story; and it showed how the humans had changed the dinosaurs by giving them a gift—humor.

"Project Fear" set up conquering a hostile planet as the main conflict. The "thing" on the planet D'Maan was a single lifeform that lived in the planet's waters. It could detect the electromagnetic fields generated by other lifeforms, and its first line of defense was to bring one's fears to a conscious, visible level. However, it also had other defenses, including the ability to disintegrate matter.

After discovering how colonists could protect themselves against the "thing" (a blanking field that neutralizes one's electromagnetic field), the troubleshooting job was over and the main conflict resolved. The trailer accomplished three things. First, it allowed me to perform a roll call of sorts to let the reader know who was still alive. Second, it resolved the viewpoint character's secondary conflict, being accepted by the other members of the troubleshooting team. Third, and most important, it showed the true motivation of the team leader, Miklynn, in taking on the planet and in the manner that he did. Recall that in setting up the story situation it was established that Lua and the Arapeth would be doing the followup work on the planet D'Maan, and also that Lua was responsible for getting Miklynn thrown out of the Terraform Corps some years before. The following scene finds Dean in a hospital bed . . .

I held up my head. "Miklynn, what about the followup, and what was Parks laughing at?"

Miklynn held out his hands, shrugged, then let his hands drop to his sides. "Lua and his combine will be the so-called followup on D'Maan. Understand about Lua; he's the Arapeth equivalent of a robber baron. As soon as he puts down, he'll have his crews out stripping the planet bare for anything and everything he can get his grubby claws on." Miklynn grinned, and I swear canary feathers were sticking out of the corners of his mouth. "Those blanking fields will work fine as long as they don't do anything but walk around. But when they begin processing materials—" He shrugged, then chuckled. "I had a few suggestions for the followup regarding water pollution, but Lua wasn't interested." He stood, nodded, then left, followed by Jerzi.

I folded my hands and pondered the confrontation between the environmentally ignorant Arapeth and water that could fight back. I nodded. Red Miklynn had licked the planet that he was after: Arapeth.

In other words, the trailer recast the meaning of the entire story. "Instead of a twist ending, it was a twist story" as one reader put it. The trailer also gave the reader a strong insight to Miklynn's character. As the character Dean observed: . . .

Some months later, up to our ears in another project, I asked Red if he thought revenge was a proper way for someone of his talents to spend his time. He thought upon it for a moment, then looked at me.

"How else do you get back at somebody?"

SEAMS

In designing and constructing the parts of your story, it is vital that the joints or seams between the parts do not stand out, signaling to the reader that a story is being told. Joining the parts together in the least obvious way possible is done through transitions and blending.

Transitions are devices that lead the reader from one situation, viewpoint character, premise, setting, time, etc., to another without either losing the reader or making the change an obvious exercise of storytelling mechanics. The transition is actually a mechanism for hiding other mechanisms.

You have just concluded a scene and are about to begin the next scene. *Something* must have changed—a different viewpoint character, a different setting, time has passed—otherwise the original scene should continue. What are the changes? Have those changes clear in your mind, then begin the next scene by putting those changes up front for the reader. Just as with the beginning of a story, with the beginning of a scene the reader must know who, what, why, when, where, and how. Otherwise, the reader may become lost and you may show the joints of your story.

For example: In the year 2233, John awakens in Dallas, Texas from his deepfreeze sleep and confronts the new society that exists there. End of first scene. If you want to maintain John as the viewpoint character, but want to skip ahead in time, the next scene might begin with: The next day, John . . . If you want to switch viewpoint characters, the next scene might begin with: Aardaak turned from the monitor and spoke to his assistant. "Jerak, that creature John must be watched . . ." If you want to change locations, the next scene might begin with: John frowned as he observed the skyline of New Mars . . . If you want to change all three, the next scene might begin with: The next day Aardaak turned from the monitor, rested his gaze for a moment upon the skyline of New Mars, then spoke to his assistant. "Jerak, that creature John must be watched . . ."

The opening transition in a new scene—however it is worded—has one function: to inform the reader about whatever is different from the previous scene. This relocates the reader firmly into the story and you may proceed from there.

Seams between scenes are more easily troweled over than are the spaces between major story parts. As was discussed in the first chapter, the character situation must include a character, his motivation (goal), and the setting. All of this takes place within one scene. The following example shows seams:

June 14th, 2414. Arlo Stumpneggle wanted that diamond, and he didn't care how he got it. It was on the planet Gemzzs; a hot and dusty place . . .

The parts above (time, character, setting) stick out. The same information can be conveyed to the reader without exposing your joints. The process involves mixing the parts such that it is difficult to tell one from the other. This process is called "blending."

"What . . . what day is it?" Arlo Stumpneggle weaved against the heat radiating from Gemzzs' dusty surface and pulled the journal from his pack. As he pulled it free, his quarter-full canteen sloshed, reminding him that all he needed to do to relieve his parched lips . . . no!

No! Arlo squinted his eyes against the glare, trying to make out the scrawl on the page. *June? Was it June? June fourteenth of a far distant, foreign time designation: 2414.* He dropped the journal to the sand. "There is no time . . . not here." He moved his feet toward the tall dunes.

EXERCISES

1. Where in your story should you look to find an appropriate title?
2. What do you have to identify in your story to find an appropriate title?
3. How do you "force" a title?
4. What should you do with titles that have no stories? Why?
5. Where in a story is the buildup found?
6. What is a saga?
7. What are the most important story features of the saga?
8. What is the difference between a saga and an adventure?
9. What is an escape story?
10. What is pacing?
11. How should both adventure and escape stories be paced?
12. How do horror and terror stories fulfill their purposes?
13. Through what vehicle do horror and terror stories achieve their effect?
14. What is the difference between horror and terror stories?
15. What kind of pacing is most effective in horror and terror stories?
16. What is the main character goal in a mystery story?
17. What are the three types of plants (clues) necessary to the mystery story?
18. What are the purposes of the three kinds of plants (clues) in a mystery story?
19. What is the difference between a mystery story and a puzzle story?
20. What is the difference between a puzzle story and a "tomato surprise"?
21. What is a "bright moment"?
22. What is a "dark moment"?
23. What are the two main purposes of bright and dark moments?
24. What is a plant?
25. What is "sucking in the reader"?
26. How are plants used to prepare the reader to accept an improbable situation?
27. What is the danger in inserting plants that are not used?
28. What is a twist ending?
29. How are plants used to set up the reader for a twist ending?
30. What three things must an ending accomplish?
31. What is a "trailer"?
32. What are seams?
33. What are used to hide seams between scenes? How are they used?
34. What is used to hide seams between story parts? How is it used?
35. On the next page are the components of a story situation. Using these components, keeping in mind the story hook, write the story's opening scene using blending to avoid showing the scene's joints:

Character: Damon Fannon, a human sociologist/historian from the year 2666 whose principal instrument of investigation is time travel.

Characterization: Fannon is an ivory-tower academic who has never experienced crime or brutality in any form. His society is nontheistic but he finds the notion of religion somehow dreamy and romantic.

Original Character Goal: To gather first-hand information on this phenomenon called "religion" by living among the people of ancient Greece in the time when gods made their home on Olympus. However, his new goal is to get back to his own time because:

Obstacle: Something goes wrong with his time vehicle, and he knows not what.

Setting: Outside the U.S. Embassy, Teheran, Iran, September 15th, 1979 (the middle of Ramadan).

Main Conflict: Fannon is identified as an infidel and mistaken for an American. The scene ends with Fannon being pursued through the streets of Teheran by 20,000 screaming *Shi'ite* fanatics bent on tearing Fannon limb from limb for the greater glory of the *Imam*.

CHAPTER FIVE

POINT OF VIEW

Who is going to tell your story? This is one of the more important considerations in fiction writing, since a different story will result depending on who tells it. The story's purpose, structure, characters, length, and a number of other things too numerous to mention will lean the choice of story viewpoint in one direction or another. The "eye" through which the happenings in a scene or story are observed is called the scene or story's "viewpoint." If the eyes belong to one of the the characters, the character is called the viewpoint character or point of view character (P.O.V. character, for short). Character viewpoint is to be distinguished from non-character viewpoint. So-called camera eye narrative, in effect, tells no story but lets the reader observe one taking place. In a manner of speaking, this would make the reader the viewpoint character. With third person omniscient narrative, the author tells the story, becoming the piece's viewpoint character. Changing from one viewpoint or viewpoint character to another is called "viewpoint shifting." All fiction viewpoints are expressed through narrative form.

NARRATIVE FORM

After subtracting quoted dialog from a story, the remainder is "narration." Fiction narration falls into four general groups: First person (character telling his own story); Second person (making the reader a character in the story); Third person, or "omniscient narrator" (the author telling the story from a viewpoint that can know and see all, past, present, and future); Limited third person (the author telling the story, but from a viewpoint limited in some manner. For example, it may be limited to one viewpoint character per scene, allowing sight into more than one character's head only through scene changes; or the entire story may be limited to a single viewpoint character. A further limitation is the "camera eye" which allows sight into *no* character's head. It is as though a television show were being watched with a character's thoughts and motivation shown only by what that character says and does).

Two narrative variations are synoptic narrative (camera eye presented as a factual history lecture), and documentary narrative (stories presented as a letter, series of letters, or other documents. The documents can take any narrative form or combination of forms).

First Person Narrative

Example from: **"Enemy Mine"**

Damn, but it worked on me. Escape from the planet had been out of my thoughts, had been buried, hidden for all that summer. But again, it twisted at me. To walk where a sun shined, to wear cloth again, experience central heating, eat food prepared by a chef, to be among . . . people again.

I rolled over on my right side and stared at the wall next to my mattress. People. Human people. I closed my eyes and swallowed. Girl human people. Female persons. Images drifted before my eyes—faces, bodies, laughing couples, the dance after flight training . . . what was her name? Dolora? Dora?

I shook my head, rolled over and sat up facing the fire. Why did I have to see whatever it was? All those things I had been able to bury—to forget—boiling over.

"Uncle?"

I looked up at Zammis. Yellow skin, yellow eyes, noseless toadface. I shook my head. "What?"

First Person Narrative: Discussion

The main advantage to first person narrative is that every aspect of the character doing the narration can be deeply and convincingly explored. Since the purpose of "Enemy Mine" was to show how the story's events affected and changed the character of Davidge, first person narrative was chosen. In the scene fragment above, Davidge, after almost accepting his situation and after developing a grudging love for the alien child Zammis, lapses into despair and momentarily focusses his despair in the form of hatred for the child, then discards the feeling. The subtlety of this change would be almost impossible to show convincingly through any other narrative form.

First person narration has several severe disadvantages that makes it useless in certain types of stories. First, with this form of narration, you are stuck with the narrator as the viewpoint character: all you can depict and all that you can show the reader is what the narrator perceives, feels, and understands. This limits both the suspense to be achieved through threats unknown to the character (you cannot depict them as threats until the character perceives them as threats), and it limits the complexity of plots allowed through the use of multiple viewpoints.

Second, you are forced to make the narrator the character with whom the reader must identify, which limits the types and degrees of characterization you can use; few readers will willingly identify with a no-saving-graces, 100-percent corrupt villain. On the other side of the coin, few readers will willingly identify with a narcissist; your character may be brave, heroic, handsome, and loyal, but he cannot say this about himself.

Second Person Narrative

Example From: **"Made Up"**

You sit alone in that room. Perhaps you feel a slight breath on the back of your neck? Do not be concerned. Many have felt it. This house beds many spirits. Oh? You *don't* pay mind to such nonsense? Well . . . it's your neck.

How does your chair feel? Comfortable, I hope. Of *course* I do. I care not what fools call me; I am no fiend. Remember that as you turn these pages; as you sit in this room; in this house. My entertainments might appear—to some— bizarre, even macabre. But I am no fiend. Evil is my entertainment, not my obsession.

Perhaps you should work your arms around. I think you might be developing a cramp. Nothing important just tension. No? Not to concern myself? *Nothing* scares you? Well . . . keep sitting there, and we shall see . . .

Second Person Narrative: Discussion

Second person narrative form makes the reader an active character in the story. In theory, this form of narrative has the potential to increase reader involvement and identification. In practice, however, the author using this narrative form risks losing reader credibility. The reader *knows* he is not a character in the story; attempts to force the reader to become a story character, therefore, appear clumsy—unconvincing. For this reason, second person narrative form is rarely used in modern fiction.

An easy mistake to make (which I do every so often) is to confuse second person narrative *form* with second person narrative *address*. Second person narrative form makes the reader an active story character; second person narrative address has the narrator talking directly to the reader, but does *not* require the reader to become a story character. The following example, from my story "Dreams," uses second person narraive address. This form of address was used to look in credibility and reader involvement through a pseudo nonfiction scenario. The actual narrative form, of course, is first person.

Example From: **"Dreams"**

. . . Let me sprinkle the pieces of my broken rule before you. They are dreams I have, yet . . . they are something else. They are where I have been, they are the experience I draw upon to write, they are nightmares to the nth power that let me meet the horrors all of you laugh off with the morning sun and try to describe to bored listeners at the breakfast table. They are dreams, I am sure; that they are *nothing but* dreams, I cannot tell. No one can.

Let me tell you about when they started. . . .

Third Person Omniscient Narrative

Example From: **"Peacemaker"**

Milton Stitch reached a hand underneath his gray and silver pin-striped coat and scratched vigorously at the peacemaker surgically implanted beneath his left breast. A rash was developing and the damned thing needed tuning, which meant being late for work again. Withdrawing his hand, he pushed open the lobby door and marched outside. He found the doorman leaning against the building calmly watching the cars go by.

You lazy nigger; get off your butt and get me a cab! "Good morning, Mister Wyler. Would you call a taxi for me, please?"

The doorman returned Milton's glance, and looked at the line of cabs waiting in front of the apartment complex, then looked back. *What's the matter, jewboy? Too good to call one for yourself?* "Yessir. I'll have one directly."

The doorman pushed himself away from the wall, moved to the edge of the sidewalk, and motioned to the first cab in line. The cab moved up, the doorman opened the door and looked at Stitch. *Well, yid, do I have to fold you up and stuff you in?* "Here you are, Mister Stitch."

Stitch reached into his pocket and flipped the doorman a quarter. *Here; go buy yourself a slice of watermelon.* "Thank you, Mister Wyler."

Wyler glanced at the quarter. *Cheap hebe honkey.* "Thank you, Mister Stitch, and have a nice day." He closed the door.

The cabbie looked back through the wire mesh at his passenger. "The Techarts Building, please."

Lousy kikes have all the money. A cab to go four lousy blocks! The cabbie smiled and turned to the front, dropping the flag. "Yessir."

Third Person Omniscient Narrative: Discussion

"Peacemaker" never sold for reasons that are probably obvious; the literature is still kind of touchy about certain issues. Nevertheless, this story is the only one I know of where I ever allowed sight into more than one head per scene; and that was because it was the only way to demonstrate how the "peacemaker" worked: a person can say anything he wants, but it comes out only in socially acceptable forms.

The advantages in using the omniscient narrator are that the narrator can peek into as many minds per scene as desired, can relate the past, and is fully acquainted with the future ("little does our hero know that tomorrow . . ."). The disadvantage to the omniscient narrator is risking reader credibility. Who is it that can peek into all these minds at will, and who also knows the past, present, and future in detail? If the reader asks this question, you are in trouble because the answer is: the author. That's when the reader stops living the story, begins being told a story, then puts it down and looks for something else with which to occupy his time. Which brings us to "show and tell" problems:

Show & Tell

The omniscient narrator must be watched carefully, for it is the chief culprit in "show and tell" errors. The rule is to *show* the events of the story taking place. The omniscient narrator *tells*. Looking over the stories I have published, I have found several occasions where I lapsed from limited third person into using an omniscient narrator; telling instead of showing. For example, in **"SHAWNA,**

Ltd." appears the following (omniscient narrative—telling—is in italics):

As the huge, swept-wing liner taxied out to the run up pad at the end of the runway, Enoch Rawls began wishing he had never taken up Leonid Veggnitz's offer. *The brain behind SHAWNA, Ltd. had coaxed the semanticist into converting the premises and applications of SHAWNA theory and flight from Aristotelian to Non-Aristotelian logic. "Soup it up," as Veggnitz had put it. The philosopher pilots he had seen in the cockpit looked competent, but Enoch Rawls had never been up before.* As the engines grumbled, he turned to his right. Captain Sanford, director of the spaceline's philosophical flight school, looked back. "Is there something the matter, Doctor?"

"Captain, why does this ship have engines? I thought all we had to do was think our way to Betelvane."

Do you see the difference between showing and telling? The parts in the example above *not* in italics are *showing* the reader what is taking place in the story. The part in italics is the author stepping on the page and talking directly to the reader. In the example above, it was sheer laziness: I had a wad of backfilling to do and not much space in which to do it. With a little more work, the same information could have been conveyed by showing Rawls thinking, or through conversation between Rawls and Sanford.

In the next example, from **"The Magician's Apprentice,"** it simply slipped by me—I didn't notice that I had done it until after the story had been published (again, omniscient narrative is italicized):

Yudo and his two brothers stood looking at their grain field. *Green only the day before,* it now lay brown and withered. Yudo nodded. "It is the power of Rogor. Your tongue angered him, Arum."

A small thing? Perhaps. But it still detracts from the story. How do we (the readers) know that the field was green the day before? We weren't there yesterday to see it; none of the characters thought it or mentioned it. How do we know? We know because the author is *telling* us, that's how. In a story two things should *not* be apparent to the reader: the mechanics of the story and the author of the story. Removing the author from the example above is easily accomplished:

Arum looked up from the withered grain stalks in his hand and turned to his two brothers. "These were green only yesterday!"

Yudo nodded. "It is the power of Rogor. Your tongue angered him, Arum."

In the example below, from **"Homecoming,"** backfill laziness once again had me telling instead of showing:

Baxter caught a flash of a sign, "ODQ-D7," recalling Deb's comment when she first saw it. "This is our new home? Oh, I like the name; it's so much nicer than Hollywood Hills or Sutton Place." He snorted and leaned on the accelerator as he came abreast of the parking ramp for the experimental aircraft. Deb was ready with a comment for that, too. "Oh, what a nice view—Baxter, I want a divorce!" *She didn't really, but she was not happy, and neither was Baxter. An experienced test pilot, he had left the Air Force during the testing cutbacks of the late sixties to begin his own advertising agency. As a reserve officer, he had assumed that, if he ever was called up, it would be as a pilot. But the Air Force had found his advertising skills much more desirable, and dropped him in public relations.* Baxter glanced out of the side window at the black, needle-pointed craft on the ramp being readied for a test. "Dammit, it is a beautiful view!"

The lapses in the three examples above are brief, they did not happen frequently, hence they were tolerable enough not to make their stories terminal. This does *not* mean that such tolerable lapses into telling either can or should be used. They are errors. As a writer you will want more of a reaction to your writing from the reader than tolerance.

Limited Third Person Narrative
(Single Point of View)

Example From: **"The Portrait of Baron Negay"**

"We take the fingers off of forgers, Tomasi." The baron grinned around the horrors he used for words. "Then we burn them, using the ashes to make my fields more fertile."

Tomasi held out his hands. "As well you should, Excellency."

The baron turned to his right and nodded at the old man, then returned his glance to Tomasi. The old man pulled a coder from his pale yellow robe and moved to the painting. "Old Peter will examine the work. He is our resident expert."

Tomasi met the old man's glance, then held out his left hand toward the painting. "The great Sabro and I have nothing to hide."

Old Peter reached out his right hand and touched the paint. Tomasi recognized expert fingers feeling the texture and dryness of the work's surface. The forger's expression was one of genuine unconcern. *I am an expert, too, old man.* The forger smiled as Peter turned and faced Baron Negay. "The composition, style, technique, period, and medium appear to be Sabro's, as do the choices of canvas and frame." He looked back at the painting and lifted his coder. He drew the small red box across the face of the painting, read the numbers that appeared in the coder's tiny screen, then replaced the box in his robe. Tomasi frowned as he saw the same hand withdraw a pocket art register. *These fools have already been burned.*

The old man flipped through the pages of the register, then stopped. He studied the small book, then turned to the Baron. "Excellency, the work may be genuine. The magnetic code number matches that of Sabro's missing work entitled 'Hands.'" He turned toward Tomasi.

"However, this work is recorded as having been destroyed in a Yorkshire fire. This piece may be a forgery—an excellent forgery—but still a forgery."

Tomasi smiled. "My dear Peter, the great artist himself was killed in that fire. The register only shows works that had been registered as sold prior to Sabro's death, along with the few that have been turned up since in the colonies." Tomasi again placed his hand on the frame. "I assure you that this painting is as genuine as the others that have been authenticated since the fire." Tomasi nodded. *I know; I forged those too.*

Limited Third Person Narrative
(Single Point of View): Discussion

Everything in this story is seen through the eyes of one character: Tomasi the forger. We can see his thoughts (italicized portions of the text), but we cannot see anyone else's thoughts. Why use third person narrative limited to a single viewpoint rather than first person narrative? At the point in time in which the scene fragment above takes place, Tomasi is both a criminal and a quite cynical character. Limited third person narrative allows the reader time to become acquainted with the character and his motivations before deciding to identify with him. In addition, storytelling (what Tomasi would have to be doing to present this in first person), is out of character for the forger. He is a forger of paintings, hence words would not be his first choice for a medium of expression. In addition, criminals are not noted for being chatty.

Another reason for using limited third person (instead of first person) is because later on in the story Tomasi is affected by his experiences, becomes a better person, and goes on to perform a heroic task that helps to bring down an entire empire. Again, these are not the sort of things a character can say about himself without patting himself on the back. Limited third person is more detached than first person and can, therefore, explore the viewpoint character's positive qualities with less peril.

A single viewpoint character per story, however, does have the same plot complication restrictions as first person narrative. Threats unknown to the character cannot be perceived as threats until the character perceives them.

Limited Third Person Narrative
(Single Point of View Per Scene)

Example From: "Savage Planet"

As he approached the first encampment, Michael Fellman saw twelve young females competing to see which of them would have the strength, courage, and stamina to become males. Michael remembered a line from the report: *The Benda cannot conceptualize an organization beyond the family level. It appears, then, that the company must either treat with separate families—with the entailing impossible conflicts inherent in such arrangements—or devise a plan that will enable the Benda to be treated as a unity, or eliminated completely.*

Michael shook his head at the frigid sense of purpose implied by the report. The cynicism of pragmatics brought to the ultimate cynicism: the elimination of a race to achieve the kind of political stability that would attract investment capital to the RMI coffers. . . .

Armath waited at the auditorium door for the opening to clear. At a break in the ingoing traffic, Armath spaced himself behind the most recent entry the customary four paces, then moved into the huge, vaulted structure. Its size was necessary to seat the Benda students in such a manner that no two of them came any closer than four paces apart. Armath moved down the ranks, spotted an open place, then walked to it and squatted on his four walking hands, facing the tiny stage at the front of the room. . . . Armath bowed his head, sighed and waited. After a few moments, the auditorium grew silent. The frail, gray human called Fellman entered at the front of the room and climbed up on the stage before them.

He placed his papers on the lectern, adjusted the microphone, then looked at the assembled males. "Humans will bury you." The words echoed throughout the auditorium. Armath frowned, for the human's style had changed. "If this were a classroom full of humans, there would be talking, laughing, playing about. But not with *you*." Armath could feel the scorn washing from the lectern across the students. "You *can't* talk with your neighbor, can you? Look at you. Look at yourselves squatting as though each one of you was an island unto himself." Armath looked and saw the other Benda males also looking around.

"Do any of you know why you sit apart like that? I'm asking a question. Do any of you know?"

Armath stood. "It is our custom."

Fellman nodded. "How is it that it became a custom? Can you answer that?"

Armath held out his hands. "It has always been so."

The human motioned with his hand. "Sit back down." He looked over the audience for a long moment, then fixed one of the males in the front row with his eyes. "You!" The student stood. "Why are we speaking my language—the language of humans?"

The Benda frowned, then shrugged. "Our own language is not . . . it is not complex as is yours. Our only need of language is to care for our *Dishah*. We needed nothing more before the humans came to Bendadn."

Fellman nodded. "And we *are* here, aren't we? And you will die because we came—because we are *better* than you!"

Armath swallowed as the last echoes of the human's challenge faded. Inside his chest he felt a tightening. The human walked from behind the lectern, then went from one end of the stage to the other, looking over the students. He returned to the lectern and leaned his arms on it. "The custom of separation dates back before the earliest memory of your oldest. Before the custom, a male chancing to meet another male would enter combat to see who was the stronger." Fellman nodded. "Of course, you know what happened to the loser. You know because it's happening to all of *you!*"

The tightening in Armath's chest grew, and he recognized it to be anger . . .

RMI Project Manager Jacob Lynn leaned back in his chair and nodded at the biologist. "All right, Hyman. You've had a look around. Now tell me why things are not following the projections in your report."

Hyman pushed a thin wisp of brown hair from his watery blue eyes. "It's your boy Fellman."

"Fellman?"

Hyman nodded. "He's made the entire *Manifest Destiny* program into a laughing stock. In addition, he has the Benda males discussing matters that should be far beyond them. Extremely dangerous matters."

Lynn frowned. "Such as?"

"He's got them talking philosophy, politics, revolution, for example."

"What?"

Hyman nodded. "In addition, none of the males I've observed have reverted. By now they should have stopped reproducing altogether. Somehow Fellman has convinced the Benda that they are, if not superior to humans, at least not to be dominated by humans. I'm afraid that simply removing Fellman and the other teachers who are helping him will not reverse the process. The damage is done."

"What do you suggest?"

Hyman sighed, then shrugged. "There appears to be little alternative. You must convince the Benda—once and for all—that they are inferior. And this must be done in a manner understandable to the Benda."

Lynn rubbed the back of his neck. "What are you suggesting?"

"A confrontation. A demonstration of force." Hyman smiled. "I'm certain that you can devise a pretext that will satisfy the Ninth Quadrant Supervisory Forces."

. . . (Hyman continues) "One thing."

"What's that?"

"Fellman and his bunch must not leave the planet. Since they are aware of the report, it wouldn't do to have them wandering around Earth, talking." Hyman stood and walked toward the door. He paused and looked back. "There is an alternative—but I suppose you know that."

"Know what, Hyman?"

"If Fellman's efforts result in a unified Benda race, RMI will have a political entity with which to deal for minerals. It will cut into the profits some, but no more than on any other planet RMI has invested in."

"I'll be getting in touch with you later, Hyman." The biologist nodded and left the office . . . .

. . . (Lynn calls one of his mining crew chiefs) "Thorpe, I want you to have a full crew move into the Javuud Valley tomorrow. I want full scale production to be reached within the next two weeks."

"Yes sir, but the transfer of mineral rights hasn't been completed."

"Let me worry about that. And, Thorpe?"

"Yes, Mr. Lynn?"

"I'll be having a full security company with your crew for protection."

"Is there a need? I mean, has there been some trouble that I should be aware of?"

"Just taking precautions." Lynn cut off the communication, then stared at the door through which the biologist had left. Lynn's eyes narrowed as he clenched his fists. "It's not profits, Hyman. It's *Fellman!*"

Limited Third Person Narrative (Single Point of View Per Scene): Discussion

In the fragments from three different scenes above, multiple viewpoints are presented (Michael Fellman, the alien Armath, and Jacob Lynn); but they are limited to a single viewpoint per scene. This limitation avoids the credibility problems inherent in omniscient narrative. But why have more than one viewpoint? First, there are three stories in "Savage Planet." Michael Fellman, a history professor, is a man of compromise faced with a compromise he cannot accept. Armath is a member of a barbaric race that must either change almost everything in which it believes, or become extinct. Jacob Lynn, the project manager, is another man of compromise whose self-image (not to mention his job) is threatened by Fellman's belated burst of integrity.

Fellman's moment of truth, where he decides to draw the line and fight Lynn, cannot be shown with the proper effect unless he is the scene's viewpoint character. To make the Benda more than a herd of frightening thug-critters, the reader must get into one of their heads to see the things a Benda believes, values, and must change to survive. The story does not work at all unless the reader is rooting for the survival of the aliens. This requires a Benda viewpoint character. Lynn's moment of truth, where he realizes that the validity of his entire life depends upon Fellman's destruction, requires Lynn to be a viewpoint character.

The presentation of plot complexities also required multiple viewpoints. The stunt Lynn engineers to destroy the Benda and Fellman could be conveyed through a single viewpoint, but it would require either a much longer story (enabling Fellman, for example, to put together on his own bit-by-bit the pieces of Lynn's plan) or through lengthy explanations. Either option would have made the story too boring to write, much less read—or buy.

Limited Third Person
(Camera Eye)

Example From: **"The Initiation"**

Dino Gitaglia wiped the bead of perspiration from his upper lip, then looked nervously at the *soldato*, DiPalermo, standing at his side.

DiPalermo returned the look, then let his swarthy, scarred face break into a broad grin. "Hey, *compagno*, don't worry." He nodded toward the hand-carved double doors. "You'll do fine in there." They stood in silence for a few moments, then DiPalermo sighed, shrugged, and laughed. "What do you think of the Yorkers this season?"

Dino Gitaglia shook his head. "I don't follow the Yorkers." He smiled. "Put me down for the Yankees."

DiPalermo nodded. "Good. The Chief will like that. Respect for tradition."

"Checking up on me?"

DiPalermo shrugged, then patted Gitaglia on the shoulder. "Just asking. How do you think the Yankees will do in Twenty-fourteen?"

Gitaglia shrugged. "Who knows? It was a dumb move trading Vitelli."

The double doors opened, and the one called "the Irishman" leaned through and looked at Gitaglia. Then he looked at DiPalermo and cocked his head toward the open door. DiPalermo took his companion by the elbow and steered him toward the open door. "This is it, *compagno*. Just stay cool."

As Gitaglia entered and was ushered to a chair against the wall, he looked at the faces seated behind the grand banquet table. He recognized Johnny "Three Fingers" Provacci, Frank Manterro, and Joey Capuzzi. Seated in the center was Don Salvatore "The Chief" Callace. Don Salvatore nodded in his direction, and Dino nodded back.

The Chief pushed himself to his feet and held out his arms for quiet. Instantly the room hushed. Don Salvatore lowered his arms, pulled the stub of a cigar from his mouth, and dropped it into an ashtray. Grasping a coat lapel with each manicured hand, The Chief looked from one end of the banquet table to the other, then turned his eyes toward the antique cut-glass chandelier.

"This is a time of war, so I will make this short." The Chief looked down at Dino seated against the opposite wall, then held out a hand in his direction. "Look at this fine boy . . . and the other side says we are *finished!*" Don Salvatore smiled as those seated around the table laughed and applauded. They became quiet, and The Chief nodded. "Finished. Well, we almost *were* finished." He pointed around the table. "Ask Johnny there, or Frank. They remember the days when it was worth a good man's life to join." The Chief nodded. "No money, frozen out, everyone's hand turned against us, all the families at each other's throats. I can admit it now; they almost had us back in Ninety-eight. Remember, Frank?"

The one called Frank Manterro nodded. "Who could forget, *padrone?*"

Don Salvatore nodded, then made a fist and slammed it down on the table. "We lost many good friends and brothers to the . . . *maiali!*" He pointed around the table. "But, here we still are! And soon we go to the mattresses and hit them," he punched a fist into his open hand, "hard!" The Chief nodded at Dino and motioned with his hand. Dino Gitaglia stood, walked to the table, and stood across it from Don Salvatore. "Boys, this is Dino Gitaglia. He comes on Vincente DiPalermo's recommendation." The Chief studied Dino, then turned and looked at those seated around the table. "I look at this boy, and I think. We have done many things—adopted from the other side many ways—just to survive." Don Salvatore looked at Dino and smiled with a look of fierce pride. "Many said that we would *never* survive, no matter *what* we did." He nodded and held out a hand toward Dino. "But, *look!* Look at Dino Gitaglia, and tell me such as this swears his life and soul to a dying organization!"

The Chief motioned to one side and "The Irishman" walked up and placed a gun and a knife on the table between Dino and Don Salvatore, then withdrew. "Dino Gitaglia, this represents that you live by the gun and the knife," he held out a fist, "*and* that you *die* by the gun and the knife! *Comprènde lei?*"

Dino nodded. *"E inteso, padrone."*

"Cup your hands." Dino put his hands together and held them over the weapons. The Chief crumpled up a sheet of paper, placed it into Dino's cupped hands, then struck a match and ignited the paper. "Say this: this is the way I will burn if I ever betray our secret."

Dino looked up from the burning paper with unblinking eyes. "This is the way I shall burn if I ever betray our secret."

The flame died and The Chief nodded. "Never forget what I now tell you. Burn it into your mind. Betraying our secret means death without trial. Violating any member's wife means death without trial. Look at them, admire them, and *behave* with them." Don Salvatore held up his hands. "Everybody up, and throw a finger from one to five."

Everyone stood and held out one hand with one or more fingers outstretched. The Chief counted up the total, then began counting from the left end of the table, stopping on Johnny "Three Fingers" Provacci. Don Salvatore turned toward Dino. "Well, Dino, that's your *gombah*—responsible for you as your godfather."

Johnny Provacci laughed, stood up, and walked around the table, stopping in front of Dino. Provacci held out his hand. "Give me the finger you shoot with."

Dino held out his right index finger. Provacci pricked it with a pin and squeezed it until the blood ran. Don Salvatore spoke. "This means that we are now one Family." The others, seated at the table, stood and applauded. "The Irishman" reached out and handed a small leather case to The Chief. Don Salvatore opened it and pinned the badge on Dino's left shirt pocket. "Welcome to the ranks of the finest, Dino Gitaglia. Welcome to the New York Police Department."

Limited Third Person (Camera Eye): Discussion

"The Initiation" is a puzzle story. Recall that the object of a puzzle story is to place the reader in a situation where the reader must figure out what the situation is. But, you *cannot* cheat the reader. The same story done through first person would be cheating. With first person narrative, the narrator should have told us up front that he is being initiated into the 2014 version of the N.Y.P.D. Not doing so would make the piece a "tomato surprise." The same thing applies to limited third person narrative; if we can look inside Dino's skull, we should know the situation. And, of course, the all-knowing omniscient narrator would have known the situation. Not relating it to the reader would have been cheating. The only form of narration that works with this story is the "camera eye"—third person, but limited to only what can be seen and heard.

For those of you who might think the version above cheated the reader, observe the clues that were planted. Well up front, the evolutionary social premise of the story was planted: "We have done many things—*adopted from the other side many ways*—just to survive." Another plant: "No money, frozen out, everyone's hand turned against us." If you are more than twelve years old, New York City's financial situation and how it is affecting the N.Y.P.D. has been paraded before you in newspapers and through TV for years. *Barney Miller* even did an episode on it. "The Irishman" was named three times; and why not? The N.Y.P.D. has a large number of Irish-Americans among its numbers. *The Godfather* notwithstanding, the Mafia is not noted for its tolerance in this regard. And if that's not enough, Donald S. Callace, New York's Chief of Police in the story, was referred to as "The Chief" fourteen times. The leather case, the badge—the answer was being pointed to right up until the end. The Italian names? Prejudice does lead us to a false assumption or two, doesn't it? There are many Italian-Americans on the N.Y.P.D. right now; and is it *my* fault that the reader fell for a bunch of *Godfather, Valachi Papers,* and 1930's gangster film cliches?

You bet it is.

NARRATIVE FRAMES

A frame is one or more scenes, or an entire story, used as a setting for the main story. For example: a story told by one man about another man telling a story (see "The Jaren" in the chapter on Backfill); the first man's opening and closing narrations would be a "frame". This is called a first person narrative frame. Another type is the synoptic frame. This is where the opening and closing of the story consist of bogus history lectures. The documentary frame is the opening and closing of the story being excerpts from documents—texts, letters, wills, orders, records, etc. Multiple frames are frames within frames enclosing a story. Verb tense frames are frames in one narrative tense enclosing a main story in another narrative tense. Dream frames bracket the main story with dream sequences. Second person narrative as well as all of the kinds of third person narration may be used as frames for stories written in any narrative form. Half-frames (only an opening or closing frame) can also be used. An opening frame, such as the documentary half-frame used in "SHAWNA, Ltd.," might be used to establish a story's premise. A closing half-frame might be used as an epilog or trailer. Parallel frames (opening and closing frames with returns to the frame story at points within the main story) can be used to tie together a number of stories, vignettes, or story incidents.

NARRATIVE TENSE

With but rare exception, fiction narrative is done in the past tense. Readers are familiar with reading narration in the past tense and this familiarity allows the reader to forget the words and enjoy the story. But there are exceptions.

In the example from "Dreams" above, the narrative begins in the present tense. This is because the narrator is addressing the reader directly (part of the pseudo-nonfiction scenario). However, the narration soon lapses into the past tense for the main story, returning to present tense for the closing frame. In "Project Fear," present tense was used in the italic horror sequences to do two things: to make the experience more immediate; and to further separate those sequences from the main story.

Caution: The past perfect tense (He *had* seen them before) is a danger signal according to the narrative form being used. If the narrator is talking in the first or second person from the narrator's own knowledge or experience (I had been through this nonsense before)—no problem. But, in third person—omniscient or limited—the word "had" is a signal that you are *telling* rather than *showing* (see the examples under "Show & Tell" above).

SUMMARY

There are advantages and disadvantages to all narrative forms. With first person and second person narrative, the author is unlimited in the exploration of the depth of the narrator's feelings, personality, changes, and so forth. However, the author is forced to make the narrator both the viewpoint character and the character with whom the reader must identify. In addition, a character's description of his own handsomeness and heroics can get tedious and overbearing if not handled with great skill.

The author can get around these two problems with limited third person. In addition, sight can be gained (by shifting viewpoints) into more than one character's head. However, equalling the first person narrative's ability to examine the depth of a character's feelings and personality in limited third person is more difficult. It should be remembered that, as a general rule, the shorter the story, the fewer viewpoint characters one can have. In a short story, constant viewpoint shifting destroys reader identification.

All of these problems can be overcome by the all-knowing, all-seeing unlimited third person narrator. The author can explore as deeply into a character as the author wishes, and into as many characters as may enter the story. The problem is making the narration sound convincing. Unless unlimited third person narration is done with skill, the author will find the reader losing track of the story wondering what supernatural being it is that can possibly know and see all that is being told. The answer comes rapidly: the author. That is the moment when the reader stops living a fictional reality and begins being told a story; and at that moment the reader puts the story down because it no longer serves its function.

EXERCISES

Define the Following Terms:
1. Viewpoint
2. Character Viewpoint
3. Non-character Viewpoint
4. Narration

5. First Person Narration
6. Second Person Narration
7. Camera Eye
8. Third Person Omniscient Narration
9. Limited Third Person Narration
10. Synoptic Narrative
11. Documentary Narrative
12. Showing
13. Telling
14. Viewpoint Shifting
15. P.O.V. Character
16. Cheating the Reader
17. Tomato Surprise
18. Frame
19. First Person Narrative Frame
20. Synoptic Frame
21. Documentary Frame
22. Multiple Frame
23. Verb Tense Frame
24. Dream Frame
25. Half-frame
26. Parallel Frame
27. Main Story

Answer the Following:
28. Which narrative forms make the reader the viewpoint character? How?
29. What is the main characterization advantage to first person narrative?
30. What are the two main disadvantages in first person narrative?
31. In addition to the disadvantages of first person narrative, what other disadvantage is there to second person narrative?
32. What are the advantages in using third person omniscient narrative?
33. What is the main disadvantage in using third person omniscient narrative?
34. Explain the difference between showing and telling. Why should a story show rather than tell?
35. What disadvantages does limited third person narrative (using a single P.O.V. character) have that are eliminated through the use of multiple P.O.V. characters?
36. What is camera eye narrative, and how is it used in a puzzle story?
37. What is the primary use of a parallel frame?
38. Give two reasons for using the present tense in narration.
39. When can you use the past perfect tense in first and second person narration?
40. When shouldn't you use the past perfect tense? Why?
41. Story situation:
   Setting: (pick your own).
   Character: (a woman—fill in the rest).
   Characterization: (use your own).

Character goal: She is pregnant and is about to deliver; she wants very much to keep and to rear her baby.

Obstacle: In her society, to become a mother, one must matriculate at the college level, proceed to parent college, then pass an examination equivalent to a bar exam before one can either bear children or rear them. The penalty for violating these requirements is confiscation of the child and death for the mother. In the event the prospective mother is apprehended before the child's birth, both mother and fetus are exterminated.

Main Conflict: She doesn't have her credentials and is apprehended.

A. Write the opening scene of this story using third person omniscient narrative.

B. Write the same scene using third person limited narrative (one P.O.V. character).

C. Write the same scene using first person narrative.

D. Write the same scene using second person narrative.

E. Write the same scene using camera eye narrative.

F. Which narrative form was the most effective?

G. Why?

CHAPTER SIX

CHARACTERIZATION

Stories are about people. The events or settings might be weird and wonderful, incredibly technical, or downright impossible. Your entire purpose in writing a story might be to make a scientific, sociological, or political point or to show off a terrific idea; but your story must be *about* people. The people may be ordinary, next-door humans or extraordinary humans of impressive ability, accomplishment, and ideals. The people may be mutants, mental cripples, or psychotic killers. The people might be translucent blobs of slime, fields of dis-embodied energy, telepathic oceans, the creatures of religion, or even mechan-ical. But, they are—and have to be—people; without people—changeable, goal-choosing entities—you do not have a story. The people in your stories are called "characters." The form you have them take is called "characterization."

The most recent area of growth in science fiction as a form of literature is characterization. This has resulted in a number of approaches to the subject and in controversy.

SOME THOUGHTS ON APPROACHES

There are theories concerning characterization that are just as comfortable and as easily understood as Newtonian physics—and that I find just as limiting. These theories expound upon the purpose of character, the importance of character in relation to other story elements and the range of characteristics a story character should be allowed to possess. In his article, "Heroes, Heroines, Villains," in *The Craft of Science Fiction* (see "References"), James Gunn does an excellent job of collecting and explaining these theories; and it would be well worth your while to read and become acquainted with the arguments and il-lustrations he presents. The method of characterization that works for you might be there. Science-fiction characterization has been and is still being executed in the ways he describes; and such stories sell.

Gunn, for example, subscribes to a limited version of E. M. Forster's division of characters into "flat" and "round"—the flat possessing a single unchanging characteristic; the round having several characteristics, with perhaps several in conflict—sort of like people. But characterization in science fiction still leans toward "types." Some writers do this from habit; others for considered reasons.

James Gunn holds that the "point of science fiction" demands it. He states: "all characters are selected to fulfill the necessities of plot, no characters are truly unpredictable, none are truly rounded, and the best are a selection of traits. For there is a difference between science fiction characters and the characters of traditional fiction; the characters are, indeed, less rounded and more typical. The critic who fails to understand this is going to miss the point of science fiction, but the writer who fails to understand it is going to wonder why his stories are misunderstood."

He underscores his point by quoting Elizabeth Bowen's bloodless remark: "Each character is created in order, and only in order, that he or she may supply the required action." Gunn nails down the lid on this casket by following with: "Those who maintain otherwise are capable of deceiving themselves." Curses with less finality have appeared above the entrances to Egyptian tombs.

This admittedly brief summary of Gunn's views concludes with the root philosophy dictating Gunn's theory of characterization: " . . . no one reads science fiction to become better acquainted with real people; the strangeness of the situation is the drawing power of science fiction. The characters exist to react to those circumstances, to show how those changed circumstances would (or will) affect people . . . the characters are surrogates for the reader or for the human race . . . The science fiction tendency is to make the characters the creatures of the plot; in mainstream fiction, characters tend to create their own plots."

In learning how to write, the rules with which you program youself will lead you down certain paths and direct you away from others. Everyone who writes about writing hopes to point you toward the greatest number of successful paths and steer you away from unsuccessful ones. The characterization approach outlined above may be all you will ever need or want, depending on your reasons for writing. I find the approach above severely limiting; had I been programmed with those rules, three quarters of my stories never would have been written.

What works for one writer may *or may not* work for you. I find it extremely limiting to design characters as cold-bloodedly as one would design parts for a machine. In my story dump I have both characters looking for story situations and plots waiting for characters. Not far into the writing of a story, regardless of my original thoughts or plans, the characters become real to me. I do not mean imaginable; I mean *real*. And just like other real people, they tend to have their own views, goals, and ways to go about things.

I have literally fought wars with my characters. When I am smart, I eventually give in and listen to them, reconstructing the rest of the story accordingly; when I try to force them in a particular direction (after all, I own the writing machine), the story falls flat. The characters in the final draft *must* be as thoroughly integrated with theme, purpose, structure, plot, and situation *as though* they had been specifically designed to fit that particular set of story functions; but for me it is a matter of give-and-take between all of the story elements during the writing process.

Centering stories on character—using space, science, and future as settings for a story of character, instead of using character "types" as excuses to demonstrate the story's scientific wonder—is at least valid in modern science fiction, if not rapidly becoming a requirement. As with mainstream fiction, modern science fiction is more concerned with how developments and events affect characters. The more mature science fiction becomes as literature, the less the scientific gimmick can fill the lead role in your story. This is because the gimmick will be less able to carry the story; modern science fiction is but a degree away from *being* this age's mainstream fiction. Once the labels on the books and magazines change, science fiction will *be* mainstream. And, as with mainstream fiction, characters have to carry the story.

In this chapter, and in Chapter Eight, you will see more of my approach. Nevertheless, I cannot stress enough that my way may or *may not* work for you and for the stories that you want to write. There is a line from Kipling that several people in the business are fond of quoting:

"There are nine-and-sixty ways
Of constructing tribel lays
And every single one of them is right!"

SOURCES OF CHARACTERIZATION

Inventing a believable character requires three kinds of understanding: First, the character must be believable to *the reader,* and the reader will test your character's believability against the only basis for comparison that he has—the behavior the reader has observed and has experienced. This includes the behavior of both animals and plants, as well as the behavior of fictional characters. The second kind of understanding is that your only *sources* of character-building material are the same ones that the reader uses for comparison. Third, every act that we call "behavior" is caused by what we call "motivation," and every character's motivation *is* his goals. Furthermore, no one has ever invented an alien half as complex, multi-leveled, and downright strange as a human being; and humans will be the readers of your stories. If the character you build and the way it acts are not recognized by the reader, your construction will not be believed; it will not convince.

Your initial source of character-building material is yourself. Reality is a life-long first person narrative with you as the viewpoint character. You can peek into your own skull, but into no one else's. The thoughts, reasonings, contradictions, motivations, and feelings of others can only be inferred from their behavior—what they say and do. You can see and otherwise experience your own. There is a wealth of character-building material in your head. You were born and have achieved whatever age you now have. During that entire time you have learned, observed, experienced, fantasized, reacted emotionally and intellectually to the persons, objects, ideas, and events around you. You have formed countless conclusions, selected countless goals, and have programmed yourself through intention, accident, indifference, or intimidation with a maze of complex, often fragmented, often contradictory rules. But you were not simply a passive sponge of experience; you also acted, and what you wanted and were at any given point in time is why you acted the way you did.

This is all material you can use. Many times I have used parts of myself in characters or just dropped my complete self into a story as one of the characters (my bloodiest battles with story characters are with ones such as these, which tells you something about *me!*)

Your next most important sources of character-building material are the people around you. Study individual human behavior and group behavior. Ask yourself: what are the contents of character (goals, values, philosophies, instincts, conditioned reflexes, experiences) behind the behavior you observe? Why does that one sit in eternal silence while that other one chatters away like a magpie on amphetamines? Why is she comfortable at a party while he looks like a trapped animal? Why did little Wilma Baker—the sweetest, quietest, most well-behaved child you ever met—slap her mother's face and run away from home?

That old woman you have a nodding acquaintance with; she's over ninety now. Her experience predates paved roads, motorcars, electric lights, flying machines, and the income tax. She remembers lace frocks, finishing schools, and coming-out parties. Her grandfather fought in the Civil War, her father chased Pancho Villa, an uncle died in the Indian Wars, a brother in the Spanish-American War, she rolled bandages for The Great World War, her son was wounded in the Second World War, her grandson died in Korea, her great-grandson deserted in Vietnam while her great-granddaughter is now in basic training learning how to quietly slit enemy throats.

What's going on behind those gray-blue eyes as they look upon a world of four billion humans? When she was ten, there was only forty percent of that number. What does she think of space travel, television shows from Jupiter, nuclear power, a world of superpowers balanced in armed terror? What does she think of the "me" generation, the assertion of individual rights by ethnic and sexual groups, the storage of old people in hives putting in a last lonely vigil before an unnoticed death? Does she think of any of it? Does she care? Try and climb into her head and look around. When you are ninety, what will your eyes see? What will you think of it? How will you feel? What will you do? *Why* will you do it?

To have a rich store of character-building material, you must become a student of human behavior, and an analyst of the behavior you observe. The things that cause smiles, frowns, blank expressions, bent backs, shrugs, angry words must be filed away for future use. A slightly raised eyebrow can mean an infinite number of things depending on the context of situation and the content of character in the being lifting the eyebrow.

Two cautions: (1) if you are the only source of characterization that you ever use, your writing will eventually become repetitious—in a word: boring; (2) the real-life characters you copy into your stories can sue the pants off you if the originals recognize but are not pleased with the reproductions. Avoid the first by going outside of yourself for character traits and behavior; avoid the second by either constructing characters from several different sources, or by making the reproduction unrecognizable to the original. A recent court decision has made clear that your camouflage had best not be superficial, all the disclaimers at the front of your story notwithstanding.

Another source of character-building material comes from animal and plant behavior. Examining this area can give you a fortune in ideas concerning both alien and future human motivation and behavior. We believe humans to be the only creatures that can choose to commit suicide. Lemmings appear to be an exception. Are they? Why do countless thousands of them periodically swim out to certain death? Study them, find the answer, take a look in your almanac at the growth rate of world population, then think of an analogous human situation. How do you build the characters? What will motivate their actions? Not all the lemmings jump into the ocean. Some stay behind. How will your characters decide who stays and who goes? How will the ones who go feel about it? Why? Are they striking out to obtain a better life, or is theirs a hopeless trek to almost certain death? If it is certain death, what motivations must you put into your characters to make the behavior of the ones who go convincing? What social environment must you create to make a character's possession of such motivations believable?

An additional source of character-building material is the fictional characters created by others. By this, I *do not* mean plagiarize the works of others. Just as real people can turn loose the dogs of law upon you for reproducing them, authors can and will do the same if you kidnap one of their literary children. But there are things you can use. For example, *I own* Mamoot, a gruff, quick-tempered little boy from the town of Arcadia on the planet Momus who is descended from a circus family of bullhands, and who also was the one who brought the great beast act back to the circus of Momus by training the Arcadian Phant Lizards. But, I do not own the name "Mamoot," gruffness, fast tempers, the concept of circus families, the occupation of bullhand, great beast acts, circuses, or lizards.

To illustrate, one character of mine is a composite of many things. Part of his outward appearance—mannerisms, as well as how he is perceived by others—is borrowed from a fictional television character. His looks and an amplification of his mannerisms come from the actor who played the television character. His true attitudes, motivations, and sense of purpose come from a sergeant I knew in the Army. His early life of orphanages, reform schools, and living on his own was taken from someone—now dead—that I knew in school. His enigmatic compassion—perceived by those who can't look into his head as anything from indifference to cruelty—comes from someone I have known since becoming a writer. His use of language comes from a military science instructor I once had—a highly literate person who delighted in breaking English rules, simply *because* they are rules.

The character I invented is a very feeling, sentimental person who is repulsed by affection or sentiment; an authoritarian figure who is in constant rebellion against authority; a man of uncompromising loyalty who derides most of all those who are loyal to him; a person who reacts first with sweeping scorn or blind violent anger, then remorse, then thought; a man to whom losing is devastating while winning is almost a non-event. These traits come from what I once was and what I now am.

None of the contributors to this character, including myself, can find their contributions in the finished product. By putting them all together, everything altered slightly—the character altered them; he is none of the above. Recalling the discussion on approaches at the beginning of this chapter, what do you think would make the more interesting story: trying to stamp this character into a plot; or letting this character take on challenges of his own invention? He is a continuing character I have used in two stories. He virtually wrote both stories, they both sold, and when he is finished testing himself, his collected tales will appear in book form.

PHYSICAL DESCRIPTION

What your character looks like to the reader can be an important clue to what kind of character you have invented. By the same token, it can be an important false clue designed to mislead the reader into judging by appearances. As a reader, I can mentally fill in the appearances of characters. In addition, at whatever pace, I want the story to keep moving. Therefore, I find solid hunks of description tedious and I have quit many books and stories simply because the authors felt the need to stop everything and throw in a few paragraphs of description. To me a story bogged down by solid blocks of description (no action) makes for tiresome reading, and the slowest story start of all is to begin with a description of a character or a setting. For my reading tastes, the author needs to put no more description into a story than is necessary to trigger my imagination.

However, some readers require fairly detailed description to get into the time and place of a story, and to "see" the characters. In addition, if the physical form of a character is vital to the story, the nature of that form must be conveyed to the reader. Still, avoid stopping the story to engage in expository descriptive exercises. Blend in the description with the action of the story. Don't *tell* the reader that Joan has blue eyes; *show* the reader Joan's blue eyes looking at something; glazed in pain; crying; doing *some*thing. Keep the story moving.

Blending action and description has an additional advantage, which is saving the reader from attacks of simileosis. The two warning signs of this disease are the overuse of the words "like" and "as," such as: "he had a belly like a bowl full of jelly," or "he was as big as a house." "He had a nose like a Roman Senator." Do you have any idea what those noses look like right now? "Her eyes were like limpid pools." Do you know what makes a pool limpid? Stagnation. This is soon followed by slime. "She had skin like a peach." Take a look at a peach sometime. Do you really want your heroine covered in that? "His cheeks were as harvest apples." An operation followed soon after, no doubt. "She felt as free as a bird." A bird is a parasite-ridden creature lockstepped by instinct and environment into a routine of attempted survival that would make an inmate of Attica feel liberated by comparison.

Similes can be useful in painting your word-picture. I've used them myself. But think up new ones, and use them sparingly. Simileosis is like alcoholism: a wee nip of the creature on holidays is good cheer and an aid to digestion; heavy, frequent use is a disease—and a bore.

SYMPATHETIC CHARACTERS & IDENTIFICATION

A sympathetic, or attractive, character is one with which the reader can identify. To some degree, the reader "becomes" one of those characters, and this is called "identification." What a particular reader will find as sympathetic depends upon that reader's background, tastes, personal experiences and so on. It is in the nature of your character's goals, strengths, and weaknesses that determines whether or not your character will appear sympathetic to a particular reader. If a character utilizes his strengths, overcoming his weaknesses, to achieve worthwhile goals, the character will be sympathetic. What are "strengths," "weaknesses," and "worthwhile goals"? The different answers to that question guarantees that no matter how you design your character, some readers will find the character sympathetic and some readers will find the character dull, wooden, even repulsive.

In any event, reader identification is vital to the success of your story. Your words must cause the reader to get on the page and "live" your story rather than sit back and read it. The difference is both profound and important. Gimmick, pun, and certain kinds of puzzle stories are less reliant upon reader identification. In most cases, they are not to be taken seriously, and you have made this clear to the reader by the type of story you are doing. On the other hand, serious stories—in both serious and humorous veins—need that identi- fication. The reader should go away from the ending of your story with blown mind, scrambled emotions, and an altered view of things. You will want the reader saying: "That was so right!" or "Wow!" or "What has this story *done* to me?" The shrug of a shoulder or "Gee, that was neat" aren't nearly as satisfying.

To obtain reader identification, the characters must be real to the reader. To make them real to the reader, they must be real to you. Write them, record their actions, research them, get on the paper yourself and "live" their lives. If you do not believe in your own characters, it will show.

CHARACTERIZATION THROUGH ACTION & DIALOG

You convey to the reader what a character is by what you show that character doing. "Doing" refers to physical movement, thought, and spoken words. In the following version of a scene fragment from my story **"Proud Rider,"** what can you tell about the characters of Captain Bostany and General Kahn?

Captain Bostany knew the perspiration running down her back was imaginary, but as she stood at strict attention before General Kahn, while he traced little circles on his command desk with a wicked- looking swagger stick, she swore her boots were filled to overflowing.

Kahn dropped the stick on his desk with a clatter, folded his arms and pursed his lips. "Let's try it one more time, Captain, shall we?"

"I . . . I await the general's pleasure."

Kahn pressed a panel on his desk, causing the bulkhead behind him to part, disclosing an activated holographic command reader. "You know what this is, I suppose?"

"Yessir."

Kahn smiled. "That will save some time. Captain, as you can see, the Ninth Quadrant Federation has enough hardware in orbit around Momus to destroy utterly any kind of force the Tenth Federation cares to send against us," the General held up a finger, "if, I repeat, if everything is functioning smoothly. With me?"

"Yessir."

Kahn picked up a sheaf of papers from his deak. "These are summary courts' records, Captain. As mission sociological officer, you will be interested to know that the Momus military mission has the worst petty disciplinary rate in the sector."

"Yessir."

"Captain, that includes the Quadrant bases around all three penal colonies!"

"Yessir."

"Captain, the men and women manning this mission are Montagnes, the most professionally disciplined soldiers in the Quadrant forces. This cannot go on. First, I want you to tell me why, then I want to know what you are going to do about it."

"Yessir. The positive soc—"

"So help me, Captain, if you start talking sociological parameters, biofeed responses, or negative poop loops again, I will eat your head off!"

In the scene above, Captain Bostany is that universe's equivalent of an ivory-tower academic being put on the carpet by an angry and impatient line officer general. He is a soldier, impatient to arrive at an answer to his problem, and he is exasperated with sociological ding-words. See how the characterization changes by altering *only* the actions of the characters, leaving the dialog intact:

Captain Bostany sighed as she slouched in front of General Kahn. The general traced little circles on his command desk with a fingernail file. She wondered when she could return to her work.

Kahn dropped the file on his desk, folded his arms and pursed his lips. "Let's try it one more time, Captain, shall we?"

Bostany awakened from a daydream. "I . . . I await the general's pleasure."

Kahn pressed a panel on his desk causing the bulkhead behind him to part, disclosing an activated holographic command reader. "You know what this is, I suppose?" His tone was definitely petulant.

Bostany grimaced, then sighed. "Yessir."

Kahn pouted. "That will save some time. Captain, as you can see, the Ninth Quadrant Federation has enough hardware in orbit around Momus to destroy utterly any kind of force the Tenth Federation cares to send against us," he swished his hand in the air, then halted the appendage to admire his well-manicured nails, "if, I repeat, if everything is functioning smoothly. With me?"

"Yessir." Captain Bostany looked toward the door, hoping for an interruption.

Kahn laid his hand on a sheaf of papers on his desk. "These are summary courts' records, Captain. As mission sociological officer, you will be interested to know that the Momus military mission has the worst petty disciplinary rate in the sector." Kahn brought his fist down upon the surface of the desk with a tiny thump.

"Yessir."

"Captain, that includes the Quadrant bases around all three penal colonies!" Kahn wrapped his arms about himself into a hug and went into pout-critical.

Bostany shrugged. "Yessir."

"Captain, the men and women manning this mission are Montagnes, the most professionally disciplined soldiers in the Quadrant forces. This cannot go on. First, I want you to tell me why, then I want to know what you are going to do about it."

God, not again, thought Bostany. She shook her head, then began again. "Yessir. The positive soc—"

"So help me, Captain, if you start talking sociological parameters, biofeed responses, or negative poop loops again, I will eat your head off!"

Easily, they are different characters, even though the dialog has not changed. Below is a rewrite of the same scene fragment, this time altering the dialog instead of the action:

Captain Bostany knew the perspiration running down her back was imaginary, but as she stood at strict attention before General Kahn, while he traced little circles on his command desk with a wicked-looking swagger stick, she swore her boots were filled to overflowing.

Kahn dropped the stick on his desk with a clatter, folded his arms and pursed his lips. "You dumb broad! You wanna try it again?"

"Ah! Oh, dear . . . I . . . "

Kahn pressed a panel on his desk, causing the bulkhead behind him to part, disclosing an activated holographic command reader. "What's that, stupid?"

"A . . . a reader?"

Kahn smiled. "*Very* good. Look, Bostany, the Ninth Quadrant Federation has enough hardware in orbit around Momus to smear anything the Tenth Federation wants to throw at us." The General held up a finger. "If nobody screws up. Get me?"

"I . . . think so."

Kahn picked up a sheaf of papers from his desk. "These are summary courts' records, Bostany. You know this mission is screwing up worse than any other unit in the sector?"

"Gud, duh . . . buh . . . "

"Captain, that includes the Quadrant bases around all three penal colonies!"

"Ah! . . . Ah, Sir. Ah . . . I—"

"Look, jerk, the grunts on this mission are Montagnes. They don't screw up—ever! What's going on, and what're you doing about it?"

"Yessir. The positive soc—"

"Don't feed me that junk. Just tell me."

Again, the characters have changed. I could run another version, changing both action and dialog, but I think the point has been made. What your characters say, think, and do—as well as *how* they say, think, and do it—shows the reader what kinds of characters they are.

QUOTATIONS

The words spoken or thought by a character or characters within a story is called "dialog." Convention holds that words spoken by mouth are to be set off by quotation marks (" "), and that each new speaker gets its own paragraph.

Because of this, it is often confusing to indent for paragraphs in the middle of a character's speech, since indentation indicates to most readers a change in speaker. If a character's speech is sufficiently long that it needs breaking into paragraphs to make it readable, the speech is probably too long. Nevertheless, paragraphs within a character's speech have only the opening quotation mark at the beginning of each paragraph. The closing quotation mark is inserted only after the guy finally shuts up. Speech quoted within speech uses single quotation marks (' ').

Words spoken by a character to himself out loud are set off by quotation marks in the conventional manner, while words thought by a character to himself can be either set off by quotation marks, set off not at all, but indicated by the narrative (he thought, etc.), or by the use of italics. In one story, I used conventional quotation marks enclosing Roman face type to indicate conversation in English, italic face type enclosed by italic quotation marks to indicate dialog in the alien language, and italic type *sans* quotation marks to show what a character was thinking.

SAIDISMS

There is a strange tribe of writers called "Saidhunters" who devote their lives to a search for "saidisms"—the needless use of the word "said," as well as useless synonyms for it (he asked, she inquired, he screamed, she whispered, he nudged, she coaxed, *ad nauseam*). If it is clear which character is speaking, dialog that ends with the exclamation mark (!) does not need an additional "he exclaimed." *That's* what the mark means! Dialog that ends with the question mark (?) does not need an additional "she inquired." Dialog that ends with a period (.) does not need an additional "he said." This is not just a matter of word economy; useless saidisms weaken character dialog. Read the following example:

John picked up the gun and aimed it at Mary. "I am going to kill you," he said threateningly.

"Kill me? *Why?*" she asked.

"Ha, ha, ha," he laughed. "Because you are *in my way,*" he responded pointedly.

"Please . . . *please,* John! I beg you! Don't kill me!" she begged.

Now, the same exchange, eliminating the saidisms:

John picked up the gun and aimed it at Mary. "I am going to kill you."

"Kill me? Why?"

He laughed. "Because you are *in my way!*"

"Please . . . *please,* John! I beg you! Don't kill me!"

The revised version may not be Pulitzer Prize winning dialog; however it is considerably more convincing than the original version. Why could the saidisms be eliminated? "He said threateningly" at the end of the first sentence repeats the obvious. The existence of quotation marks, a period, and John as the speaker take care of "he said," while the content of his remark takes care of "threateningly." We know he was talking to Mary, hence we know who was responding with "Why?" The question mark is already in the sentence. "She asked" following the sentence, therefore, serves no purpose. The tautological " 'Ha, ha, ha,' he laughed" used the descriptive action rather than the quoted speech in the revision. They both said the same thing, but laughter is more convincing if described than quoted. The obvious fact that he is answering Mary's question eliminates the need for "he responded" while the emphasis on the words *in my way* makes his response pointed. " 'I beg you . . . ' she begged," I *hope* needs no explanation.

SPEECH TAGS: WHO IS SPEAKING?

The context of the scene, description of character action, speech references, and sentence structure should provide all of the information the reader needs to know who is speaking and how the character is speaking it. Context tagging is constructing the elements of the scene such that there is never any doubt who is speaking. For example, if there is only one character in the scene, who else could be speaking? Of what possible use would be the tag: he said? Another example: there are only two characters in the scene, and you have established who begins the dialog. If you save indenting paragraphs for changes in speakers, saidisms are not needed. Still another example: Your scene has three characters, a human and two different kinds of aliens. Your human talks in correct English. The first alien speaks English correctly, but cannot pronounce the "f" sound. The second alien always speaks in the third person passive voice ("It is being thought by one that wrong he may be.")

Other kinds of context tagging can be done through the use of different type faces. A human meets a mouthless telepath:

"Move your foot!"
"Eh? What was that?"
"That was me, stupid! Move your foot!"
"Oh . . . I see. Sorry about that. Ick, you're ugly. And you sound funny, too."
"I don't sound at all. Telepaths speak directly to minds."
"Is that why your speech is *italicized?*"
"Of course. You wouldn't want the reader to think I talk the same as you, would you?"

Typeface tagging can be used in other situations, as well: one character's speech coming through a communicator's speaker might be set all in small caps. Small caps could also be used for a talking robot or computer to represent a flatness of voice tone, as well as to tag the speaker. Bold face type can be used to tag a large crowd shouting something in unison.

Action tags identify who is speaking by placing the speech immediately after a character's action. For example:

Miller scratched his beard and raised his eyebrows. "I don't know."
Owzawi sighed. "Well, I don't you think you better find out?"

Speech reference tags identify who is speaking by mentioning who is the speaker, or mentioning by name who is supposed to respond to the speech within the quoted dialog. For example (with three characters):

"My name is Filbert Jones. Are you Harry Grouser?"
"He's Grouser. My name is Buddgutt. Hey, Grouser. Whatcha think of this one. His name's Filbert."
"Filbert? You musta had one mean momma, Filbert."
"Knock it off, you two. Look, Buddgutt, how do I get out of here?"
"You don't."
"What's that supposed to mean?"
"Grouser, I don't think Filbert listens too good."
"Too bad."

Tagging the speech of your characters in the ways described above (including a mix of those methods) will eliminate the need for saidisms in most cases. However, although I have a personal aversion to saidisms, don't be afraid to use "he said" and "she said." They are widely used, invisible when not carried to extremes, and a valid form of tagging character speech.

SENTENCE STRUCTURE: HOW IS IT BEING SPOKEN?

Besides showing the reader what your character is, dialog also helps to give life to a story. For dialog to be useful in serving either function, it must be convincing. For it to be convincing, you must learn how to make those black ink marks on your manuscript sheet "sound" like the real thing. There are two problems: First, many people do not write the way they talk. In other words, they don't use the expressions, feelings, and patterns with which they are the most familiar. Stilted narration and dialog are the usual results.

The second problem is that your dialog cannot read like the real thing if it is to "sound" like the real thing. This apparent contradiction is easily proven. Tape record a conversation between two other persons. When you have the tape home, type a transcript of the conversation and read it. You won't believe what you will see: fragmented sentences, constant interruptions, incoherent word assemblies—a nightmare in type. But it made perfect sense both to the conversationalists and to you when the conversation took place. What is missing in type that made the actual conversation understandable is a wealth of body language and vocal expression. Body language, in type, is executed through the description of action. Vocal expression is executed through the use of various writing devices. In proper combination, they "sound" right; the dialog is convincing.

BODY LANGUAGE

Observe people talking. Ignore the words and concentrate on what the speaker is telling the listener with his body. Angry talk, calm conversation, evasive speech, hard sell, excited chatter, nervous whispering—all these and more have their body language counterparts. What do a person's hands do when he is trying to make a point, when he is exasperated, when he is irritated, when he is blind-mad, when he is trying to be calming? Feet tapping, fingers drumming on a table top, legs frequently crossing and uncrossing, tongue licking lips, frequent swallowing, rapid eye-blinking, eyes rapidly looking around, lip pursing, lip biting, hands clasping, hands rubbing eyes, thumbs twiddling, frequent standing, moving around, then sitting down again—it doesn't matter what words this character says; he is nervous. Perhaps close to a breakdown.

Every part of the body—and I mean *every part*—can and does show expression. Each part can speak, and both we and the readers are familiar with the language. We both speak it and listen to it every day. We see it on television, in plays, and in movies. In fact, without it, very few of the meanings we understand from our daily conversations would get through.

Take the spoken words: "I don't care." At face value (typeface value) they mean that the speaker is devoid of feelings concerning something. But what does the body say? What is the meaning of those words if they are spoken by a young girl running up to her room, tears streaming down her cheeks? What do they mean if, right after they are spoken, a glass shatters in the speaker's hand from the pressure applied to it? What it means is anything *but* "I don't care."

It would take a library to explore all the gestures, contexts, and meanings that make up "body language," and I don't propose to do so here. Neither do I plan to demonstrate all of the uses, rules, and ramifications of English as a language. I have neither the qualifications nor the space to do either. You must examine, dissect, and explore both languages through much observation, and much practice at capturing your observations on paper.

VOCAL EXPRESSION

Within the quotation marks rest the spoken words of your characters. Voice—loudness, tone, continuation—is the part of body language that you can reflect as dialog. Conventions have arisen to represent vocal expression.

Loudness: In addition to body language, loudness can be represented by (1) the use of small caps, upper case, or bold face type; (2) the use of exclamation marks, a series of such marks, or exclamation marks in combination with other punctuation marks or emphasis: "WHAT?" "What!" "What!!!" "What!?" *"What!?"* (Note that typeset upper case is much more overwhelming than upper case done on a typewriter.)

Tone: Tone is usually indicated by the emphasis (underscoring/italics) in the sentence in combination with changes in punctuation. Observe the different meanings in the following sentences:

"I am going to kill you."
"I am going to kill you?"
"I am going to kill you!"
"*I* am going to kill you."
"I *am* going to kill you!"
"I am going to *kill you?*"
"I am going *to kill* you!"

Continuation: Pauses in speech can be very significant. They can indicate thought, apprehension, fear, nervousness, frustration, or any number of other things. These depend upon where and when the pause happens, and upon its duration.

The shortest pause is the comma: "Frank, I, I don't see how we'll ever get out of this alive!" The stammer reflects, in this case, nervousness.

The next shortest pause is the long dash: "I've examined this a hundred times and—don't you see what's happening?" This abrupt change in sentence subject reflects frustration.

The next shortest pause is the ellipsis. "Water . . . water . . . " The speaker is thirsty and about ready to drop. For longer pauses, you should fall back into narrative: he paused; he paused for a long moment; he stood, silent, watching her.

Other conventions are as follows: When a speaker lets a sentence trail off without completing it, use . . . " (remember to space between dots and between the last word and the first dot);

If the sentence trails off, but is complete, do this. . . . "

If the sentence is interrupted, use the long dash—"

"—if the interrupted sentence is continued, begin with the long dash. Do not space between a quotation mark and the mark it encloses.

LANGUAGE, DIALECT, PROFANITY & THE ALIEN

For the dialog in a science-fiction story to be convincing, the language spoken by the characters must be consistent with everything else in the story. Remember that language is the most rapidly evolving aspect of the human species; that the English spoken five hundred years from now will be as foreign a tongue to the English of today as is the English that was spoken five hundred years ago. Bear in mind that current language reflects current experience, and that a lecture or barroom scene placed in time a thousand years from now will not sound at all similar to their present-day counterparts. However, don't get carried away; your English of tomorrow will be read by today's readers.

Observe the radical differences in structural forms (grammar) between the different human languages. Consider the subtle differences in meaning between almost equivalent words in English and German or Greek—that much poetry and other forms of literature "lose something in the translation." And we are all humans on the same planet. Therefore, when you stick words in your alien's mouth (or other opening), try not to have them coming out sounding like a bad imitation of a 1943 Hollywood Tojo.

Dialect is the spelling of words in quoted conversation in a fashion designed to reflect a regional variation of English or an accent. When at all possible, avoid dialect. Unless it is done sparingly and with great skill, it interrupts the story flow while the reader tries to figure out what it is that a character is saying. This can get tedious. Observe the following from Kipling's *Soldier's Three*:

" 'Twas the height av policy. That naygur man dhruv miles an' miles—as far as the new railway line they're buildin' now and again timorously, to get me out av ut. 'Dhirt I am,' sez I, 'an' the dhryst that you iver kyarted. Dhrive on, me son, an' glory be wid you.' At that I wint to slape . . . ."

The quote above is from "The Incarnation of Krishna Mulvaney," one of the funniest short stories I've ever read. But it was rough reading and slow because of the constant use of an overwhelming dialect. During the reading I wint to slape several times. In Knoxville, Tennessee I had reason to visit the University of Tennessee Hospital, where a nurse asked me: "Yawllergicanehthane?" Type has to stay on one line at a time, hence you cannot see that the last half of that enigmatic interrogative curls up to at least three lines above. Translation: "Are you allergic to anything?" Fortunately, I wasn't. Writers tend to fall in love, or gasp in horror, at the things humans do with words. I do this myself. But too often these feelings find their way into print, driving both typesetters and readers crazy.

Certain dialects can be shown better by alterations in sentence structure and verb tense rather than tongue-twisting spelling. To reflect an uneducated Southern dialect, for example, it is easier reading to write "I'm sure he done it," than to write "Ah'm sho he dunnit." The reader can take the former and mentally fill in as much of the accent as can be tolerated. Certain dialect forms (such as dropping the g and replacing it with an apostrophe) are familiar enough that they can be used with little peril. "I didn't see nothin'." There are some contractions that are easy to read, as well: "Me'n' Joe," "Better'n that." Since science fiction writers frequently encounter aliens, as well as alien speech and alien attempts at human speech, great care must be taken not to impose your literary exercises in dialect upon the reader. It is easy enough to have a translator standing by, or a character who understands the dialect and answers in such a fashion that the reader can breeze over the dialect and still know what is being said.

An important characterization language tool is profanity. Most words that are regarded as profane are slang creations of the moment with a life span of a generation at best, and a span of only a few weeks or months at worst. This applies as well to non-profane varieties of slang. In writing a story set in a future two hundred years from now, such words will have been replaced with an entirely new set. This includes profane gestures, as well. Use of such words or gestures in a society where they have long since lost their significance is anachronistic (something existing or happening at something other than its proper place or time; for example, the usage today of such past gems as "Gadzooks!" "Chicken inspector," "Twenty-three skidoo," "Drawers!" and so on).

On the other hand, there are terms of eternal duration. As long as English is spoken—in any form or derivation—I imagine that certain Anglo-Saxon terms for excrement, sexual intercourse, and parts of the anatomy will make a prominent appearance. From its origins in Middle English, which had its probable origin in Middle Dutch, the Anglo-Saxon expletive for intercourse appears to be immortal. Bear in mind that Middle English to a modern listener would sound like a completely foreign language, yet the term survived, albeit in a different form. What would a future, streamlined version be? Or, in a future where all onus has been removed from sexual acts of any kind, would the term even survive? Remember, it was and still is a useful term only because of the fear, condemnation, and embarrassment associated with sexual intercourse. It is not a "nice" thing to say; hence that is why it is said. When this condemnation no longer exists, the meaning of the term will probably change as well as its form, killing it as a "bad word."

As in the world of today, the world of tomorrow will have both its sacred cows, and its frustrations; therefore, the world of tomorrow will have its expletives. For as Mark Twain pointed out, profanity offers reliefs denied even to religion. What will that asteroid miner say after he smashes his thumb with an autohammer? Be certain that something will be said. But bear in mind two things: first, your profanity of tomorrow will be read by the readers of today, some of whom find current terms very offensive; second, (as with the overuse of any expression or language form) the overuse of profanity will tomorrow be the same thing that it is today—a character insight to an unimaginative, shallow person.

CHARACTER CHANGE

John Brunner's article "The Science Fiction Novel" in *The Craft of Science Fiction* (see "References") expresses a familiar view on change in the following manner: "There can *only* be three kinds of plot . . . they go under the most banal of names: Boy Meets Girl, The Little Tailor, and Man Learns Lesson." This is because, he states, "A human being can change in just three ways. The first is through emotional involvement with someone else. The second is by discovering something within him/herself that he/she was previously unaware of. The third is as a consequence of uncontrollable outside circumstances." Brunner's view echoes that expressed by Robert A. Heinlein in *Of Worlds Beyond* (see "References"). In Heinlein's article, "On The Writing of Speculative Fiction," he first names the Big Three, also calling them "plots." Before picking away at this, there are some terms to define.

A plot is the total of the events that transpire within a story, character change being only a fraction of those events. Boy Meets Girl, The Little Tailor, and Man Learns Lesson are more properly called "plot-themes." A plot-theme is a statement that begins the process of translating a theme into action. For example: Love conquers all (theme); Boy Meets Girl (plot-theme); John and Mary defeat all obstacles to their marriage, become wed, and live happily ever after (plot).

But is it true that a human can only change in three ways (involvement with another, self-discovery, a result of uncontrollable outside circumstances)? I can think of a fourth. How about as a consequence of *controllable* outside circumstances? What about permutations of only these four forms of change?

Emotional change, itself, can cause further emotional change, making each permutation of the kinds of change unique. There are worlds of difference between Boy Meets Girl Then Learns Lesson, and Man Learns Lesson Then Meets Girl. Because of the range of human emotions, their degrees, the multitude of ways emotions can change, and the variety of things and events that can cause change, I find it simplistic and very limiting to lump all emotional change into gross categories of Boy Meets Girl, The Little Tailor, and Man Learns Lesson. A wider range of story purposes and situations become visible to me when I think in terms of unlimited numbers of causes and forms of emotional change.

In my novelette "Savage Planet" (*Analog,* February 1980), a man of compromise finally faces a compromise that he cannot accept. He already knew that he could not accept such a compromise, and so Man Learns Lesson is out. He doesn't become a bigshot or learn anything new about himself, and so The Little Tailor is out. He doesn't fall in love, and so Boy Meets Girl is out. The circumstances are not uncontrollable, and he proceeds to prove just that. By the end of the story, his change is the formation of a new resolve—a rededication of himself to teaching truth. By stretching the definition, perhaps "Savage Planet" could be called a Man Learns Lesson piece. But if we could manage to wrestle this tale into that particular pigeonhole, would it help anyone to understand the story better, or to understand the writing of it? I can testify that it would have made writing it near to impossible.

Writing theory is not exactly a science, and I am certain that supporters of the Big Three can explain away all of my objections. Although I find that looking through the Big Three filter blinds me, many writers find it helpful to think in such terms. Find out what works best for you.

Whatever the disagreements are concerning the causes and forms of change, there is universal agreement that your story characters must change. And there are things you must keep in mind to make the changes in your characters convincing.

It would take an evolution of surgery far beyond the imaginings of any science-fiction writer to single out one emotion, then alter it without altering any other emotions within the same system. Storytellers try to do this, however; but the characters they thus create simply do not convince. Any emotional change profound enough to merit being in a story will be such that it will cause many emotional changes. For example, a man learns something new about himself. To be significant enough to serve in a story, the thing he learns cannot be a shoulder-shrugger. He must learn something deep, profound, *important* about himself. Whatever that thing is, it will do more than simply alter the content of his knowledge. What he learns might cause him happiness or pain. If it is pain, it might cause him shame to learn that this knowledge pains him, and so forth and so on through a rippling of emotional reactions, conclusions, further reactions, further conclusions until the entire emotional being at the end of the story has changed—not just one little piece of him.

EXERCISES

Define The Following Terms:
1. Characterization
2. Flat Characters
3. Round Characters
4. Behavior
5. Motivation
6. Simileosis
7. Sympathetic Character
8. Identification
9. Dialog
10. Saidisms
11. Speech Tags
12. Context Tagging
13. Typeface Tagging
14. Action Tagging

15. Speech Reference Tagging
16. Body Language
17. Vocal Expression
18. Dialect
19. What are your sources of character-building material?
20. What is the main danger in using only yourself as a source of character traits?
21. What is the main danger in using real people as characterization sources? How can you avoid this danger?
22. How can you describe the physical appearance of a character without slowing down the story?
23. What makes a sympathetic character?
24. What is the purpose of reader identification?
25. How are a character's traits conveyed to the reader?
26. What are the ways to indicate loudness in dialog?
27. How is dialog tone indicated?
28. How are speech pauses indicated?
29. How is uncompleted dialog indicated?
30. How is interrupted dialog indicated?
31. Discuss the differences between character as a function of plot and plot as a result of character.
32. Create a character, describing its traits, motivations, and background.
33. Build a story plot around the character you created in 33 above.
34. Invent a story plot requiring only one character. Invent a character to fulfill the story's plot requirements.
35. Through context and speech reference tagging, write a scene containing four characters using only dialog. In the scene, include examples of speech loudness, tone, and continuation (all forms of pauses, incompletion, and interruption).
36. Using no dialog, write a description of an angry person waiting at a bus stop. Remember to blend action and description.
37. Using no dialog, write a description of a despondent prisoner.
38. Using no dialog, write a description of a happy child.
39. Using the three characters described in 37 through 39 above, write a scene demonstrating the uses of body language, vocal expression, and all forms of speech tagging.
40. Invent ten future slang and/or "dirty" words. Provide convincing reasons (social, political, evolutionary, etc.) for both the existence and use of each term.
41. Outline or write a complete story providing the necessary story elements to make the following change of character convincing: as a result of the events that transpired within the story, J. Fargo Wells changes from a weak, sniveling failure into a strong, happy success.
42. Outline or write a complete story making convincing a reverse of the character change in 42 above (42 and 43 may be done within the same story or as different stories).

CHAPTER SEVEN

FATAL FLAWS

This chapter is a collection of a few of my rejected stories containing "Fatal Flaws." A story with fatal flaws is one that is not worth either the time nor the effort to try and repair. However, such failures should be saved because bits and pieces from dumped stories can be salvaged. Frequently several dumped stories breed in that bottom drawer and turn out a marketable work (this is discussed in the next chapter).

The offerings in this chapter cover a wide range of story problems, and it is your task to find out what those problems are. Critiques for these pieces are at the end of this chapter; but before looking at the critiques, try examining these stories and coming to your own conclusions. This will give you an editor's-eye view of the slushpile. In addition, it will give you needed experience in analyzing stories—experience you will need in reading and revising your own work before submitting it to an editor. The faults of many of these pieces can be seen by diagramming them, examining to see if all of the parts of a story are there, and if they have been done properly. Others deal with content, and at least one story brought on editorial wrinkles before the problem with the piece was discovered.

Introduction:

The best I can say about the following piece is that it seemed like a good idea at the time. The trick with **"On Hold"** is figuring out what *isn't* wrong with it. After reading it (and after you have stopped laughing) diagram it and see what is missing.

"Hold that thought."

Dzmi extended its appendage and coiled it around the gray, wriggling mass. "I am holding it, Than. See how it struggles?"

Than swam to Dzmi's side. "Let me observe." Than swam around and under the gray thing.

"What bothers it?"

"Observe, Dzmi, the thread extending away into the other. It is not mature, and we must throw the thought back."

"It is very juicy, Than." Than extended an appendage and caressed the writhing shape.

"Mmm! A grand feast for one of our kind, but not yet. We cannot wait for the thread to break."

"Can we not break it?"

"No. The other must do that, and I fear we have already upset it."

"May I not even taste it?"

"No, Dzmi. Throw it back. We must look elsewhere for nourishment."

"Doctor . . . God, it . . . it . . . "

"Calm down. Calm down and tell me what happened."

" . . . It was like . . . long, cold slithering things wrapped around my brain . . . squeezing it!"

"You are sure you can't come into my office?"

"Doctor, I'm losing my mind!" The pushbutton for line two lit on the doctor's telephone.

"I have another call. Hold that thought . . . ." But before his finger touched the hold button, the screaming began.

"Dzmi, did you break that thread?"

"No, Than. I threw it back. Observe, it still swims."

"It must be mature. We are indeed fortunate. Catch it! Catch it, Dzmi, and we shall feast!"

Introduction:

My only excuse for this piece, **"Dry Run,"** is that it was written during an extensive period of dental work that was being performed on me—work that I found less than agreeable. I suppose frequent doses of nitrous oxide can bear part of the blame. Peruse and dissect.

Lieutenant General Cornwall moaned and lowered his head gently on the dentist's couch. Clone DDS-4437B pulled up the built-in stool and leaned over the general. "If the master will open, please." Cornwall opened his mouth exposing a perfect set of transplanted uppers and lowers. "What seems to be the master's problem?" The clone deftly inserted a mirror in the general's mouth before he could answer.

"Ith!" The general pointed with his finger at his lower right canine.

"Hmmm." 4437B angled the mirror behind the transplant. "Seems to be in good shape. What did it say?"

The general pushed the clone's hand and mirror out of his mouth. "Nothing. It just hurts."

"Did you ask it?"

The general scowled. "No, I didn't ask it. I'm an infantry officer. How would it look if I walked around talking to my teeth?"

The clone nodded. "Of course, master knows almost all service personnel have had Zorik transplants. It's not at all unusual for civilians—"

"I don't see them running around talking to their teeth!" The general grabbed his cheek and moaned again. "I wonder half the time if you service medclones know what you're doing."

The clone shrugged. "Master, of course, is aware that he is under no obligation to use armed forces facilities. Perhaps a regular civilian, non-clone orthodontist—"

"I'm only a lieutenant general, not a plumber! Get on with it!"

"Yes, master. Open, please." 4437B peered inside and examined the transplant again. "The gum tissue does seem to be a bit inflamed." He reached across the general, opened a drawer, and withdrew a long, sharp instrument.

"Wuth thad?"

"Nothing to worry about, master. This is just a transceiver to let me talk and listen to the transplant." 4437B touched the sharp end of the instrument against the Zorik. "Are you all right?"

I AM WELL.

"Your host seems to be experiencing a great deal of pain. It appears to be centered in your area of responsibility."

IT'S HIS PIPE. HE USES ME TO CHEW ON THE STEM. I WANT OUT.

"Why is his gum inflamed?"

I HAD TO GET HIS ATTENTION. HE WOULDN'T ASK.

"Could you end the pain, now that we know what the problem is?"

VERY WELL. The general sighed and went limp.

4437B sat up and removed the transceiver from the general's mouth. "Master, you heard?"

"Of course I heard." The general rubbed his jaw. "I'm not giving up my pipe. Can't you get me a Zorik that can take it?"

"Some of them are temperamental." He turned to a card file and began flipping through the index. He stopped and pulled out a card. "Yes, this one might do. It's been on hard times and it will take any socket it can get."

"Is it waiting here? I'm a busy man and I don't want to come back. That's why I agreed to the transplants in the first place."

The clone pressed a button in the arm of his stool. "Send in the Zorik named Dubnood." He turned back to the general. "There should be no problem, master. You'll be out in a jif." An object came clattering down a clear plastic tube and landed on the instrument tray. 4437B touched the transceiver to the object. "Dubnood?"

YES.

"We have a socket for you, but you will be chewing on the stem of a pipe. Will that be a problem?"

NO. I'LL TAKE ANYTHING.

4437B turned to the general. "Very well, master. Open please." He touched the transceiver to the Zorik in place. "You can release now." With his forefinger and thumb, the clone pulled the transplant from its socket and placed it on his instrument tray. Then he picked up Dubnood and touched the transceiver to it. "Above gumline, you will form into a lower canine. Don't forget to let the host test his bite before you lock into form."

I UNDERSTAND.

"Open please." 4437B placed the spherical alien on the empty socket in the general's gum. It immediately took root and began to shape. "Close gently, master . . . now, open again." He touched the transceiver to the newly planted Zorik. "You may lock now, and good luck."

THANK YOU, AND THE SAME TO YOU, DDS-4437B.

The clone pushed the tray out of the general's way and adjusted the couch to a sitting position. "There you are, master. That wasn't so bad, was it?"

The general worked his jaw around. "Seems okay. Nothing better go wrong this time." The general got to his feet.

"Everything should be just fine, master."

The general snorted and marched from the room. The clone waited for the door to close, then touched his transceiver to the Zorik he had removed from the general's mouth.

EVERYTHING WORKED PERFECTLY.

"Excellent, Arzut, excellent. Why was the gum inflamed?"

SWELLING IN THE SOCKET CAUSED SUFFICIENT PAIN, BUT I EXPERIMENTED BY FORMING SPIKES AND DRIVING THEM INTO THE GUM TISSUE. IT INCREASED THE REACTION.

"Nice touch. Are you certain the pain will be enough?"

GENERAL CORNWALL WAS CONDUCTING AN IMPORTANT TRAINING EXERCISE AND DROPPED EVERYTHING TO COME HERE. AND THAT WAS JUST MY DOING. IMAGINE THIRTY-TWO ZORIKS SWELLING AND STICKING. I THINK WE ARE READY. IS EVERYTHING PREPARED AT YOUR END?

"Yes. Clones of the proper type are positioned near all critical centers of power. We have been ready a long time to end our slavery."

THEN WE ARE READY. TOMORROW AT NOON WE COMMENCE OPERATION TOOTHACHE: TWO HUNDRED BILLION ZORIKS WILL STRIKE THIS BLOW FOR FREEDOM.

"Today gums; tomorrow the world!"

Introduction:
The problem in **"Please Give"** may not leap out at you at first glance. However, it is a common problem. Two problems, actually. More like three. See if you can find what they are.

Even as I look at her, I am beginning to forget. John held his hands to his cheeks, closed his eyes, then opened them. *She is still there, but . . . God! Why can't I remember?* Long platinum-blond sausage curls hung off the edge of the bed. John pushed himself up to a kneeling position and looked at the white silk clad woman stretched out on the bed. Sleeping. John's lips trembled. "Is this . . . is this one?"

NO, JOHN, DISCONTINUE.

John moved his hands from his cheeks to his ears. "Who are you? Why don't you tell me?"

DISCONTINUE, JOHN.

John struggled to his feet, letting his hands fall to his sides. He saw the mark on the inside of her left elbow, and the other marks above. He could have no interest in this. He must discontinue. John nodded. "Very well."

He shook his head, turned and left the room. On the other side of the door, John stopped and tried to remember the girl. *Nothing.* The room. *Nothing.*

RECYCLE, JOHN.

John felt the clawing urge inside of his chest; the need. He staggered from the door, found the stairs leading down, and began stumbling toward the street. Below, on the stairs, still out of sight, he could feel one. It shimmered redly in his mind. "Is this one?"

PROBABLE. STAND BY FOR VISUAL SURVEY.

John moved down another flight of stairs. Seated in the corner of the apartment stairwell, a man in his late twenties appeared to sleep; except his eyes stared at the ceiling. PROBABILITY DECREASING, JOHN. EPIDERMAL ANALYSIS ORDERED.

John reached out his left hand and touched the bare skin of the man's arm. "Well?"

BLOOD SUGAR NEGATIVE, HEPATITIS POSITIVE —DISCONTINUE, JOHN, AND RECYCLE.

John withdrew his hand, stood and stumbled back against the railing. The filthy young man curled up in the corner of the stairwell animated his eyes and turned them in John's direction. "Man, hey . . . man, what do you want?"

John turned and fled down the stairwell. At the bottom of the stairs John burst through the open door. He leaned his back against the old brick wall, keeping his eyes pointed up in the air. *If I keep my eyes up, I won't see them.* The sky was blue with tufts of little white clouds spaced evenly between the tops of the tenements. The space before his eyes was crossed and crossed again with electrical lines, wash lines, telephone lines. *But I can't see them. I won't do it if I can't see them.*

RECYCLE, JOHN.

"No!"

RECYCLE, JOHN.

"Go to hell!"

John felt a rough hand shake his arm. "You all right, buddy?"

"Go away!"

"I asked if you were all right!"

The arm shook again. John looked down to see a man dressed in blue; silver badges on cap and chest. Reds and oranges washed before John's eyes. *Is . . . this . . . one?*

PROBABILITY HIGH. INITIATE.

The lost, clawing feeling left John as he smiled and studied the police officer. "I'm sorry, officer. Did you say something?"

The officer frowned. "Fella, are you drunk? You been snorting something?"

John shrugged. "I don't understand what you are asking."

The officer nodded. "Uh huh. Let's smell your breath, buddy."

"You are asking to smell my breath?"

The officer pushed back his cap and put his hands on his hips. "Oh, a comedian." The officer lifted his right hand and wiggled one of his fingers. John took a step toward the officer, smiled, then opened his mouth. The officer inhaled and collapsed to the sidewalk. John bent over, grabbed the officer's wrists, and pulled him into the doorway. He sat the officer up against the cracked plaster of the wall, unbuttoned and removed his uniform blouse, then rolled up the officer's left shirt sleeve. *God . . . it . . . it's starting again . . .*

INITIATE, JOHN.

John swayed for a moment as he held the officer's upper left arm and squeezed. EPIDERMAL ANALYSIS: NEGATIVE. CONTINUE. The vein stood out on the man's arm.

"What if . . . what if I don't? This time. What if I—"

CONTINUE, JOHN.

John swayed as he stared at the arm. To his mind the skin melted away leaving only a network of pulsing vessels. The clawing need grew in John's chest. He held the man's arm steady with his left hand and pointed his right index finger at the inside of the officer's elbow, spraying the skin with antiseptic. From John's middle finger, a slender, steel needle extended. John inserted the needle into the vein. Releasing his grip on the officer's upper arm, John allowed the man's blood to flow through the needle. The clawing feeling began leaving his chest, to be replaced by other feelings—sucking, whirring. As the clear fluid flowed back into the man's arm, the clawing emptiness returned. *No! Not again!*

DISCONTINUE, JOHN, AND RECYCLE.

John withdrew the needle, sprayed the tiny wound with his index finger, sealing the wound with a clear plastic coating. He let the officer slump to the floor as he retracted the needle and leaned against the doorframe. John looked outside, up, at the tiny clouds. "I never feel any better . . . why? . . . why?"

DISCONTINUE, JOHN, AND RECYCLE.

John looked down and slowly shook his head. *No . . . no more.*

DISCONTINUE, JOHN, AND RECYCLE.

Again John shook his head. He stopped, looked back at the man slumped on the floor, and saw the officer's handgun.

CANCEL, JOHN. CANCEL, JOHN.

John bent over, wrapped his fingers around the rough grip of the weapon and pulled it from its holster.

CANCEL! CANCEL! CANCEL!

He felt the hard, cold, greasy surface of the gun, then smelled the mixture of oil and solvent. In the black hole of the muzzle, John could see the ends of the spiraled lands and grooves cut into the stubby barrel. He wondered how they were made as he tightened his grip on the trigger.

CANCEL! CANCEL! CANCEL! CA—

Doctor Parvane bent over the work table and inspected John's new face. He looked up at the technician standing at the other side of the table. "Excellent, Weinblatt. Excellent."

Weinblatt shrugged as he finished wiping his hands. "Cosmetics are easy to repair, Doctor. The hard part is the neural directional unit. It was blown all to hell. Had to replace the whole thing. Expensive."

Doctor Parvane dismissed the cost comment with a wave of his hand. "It will be more than worth it if we can get a functioning prototype. I suppose we should have called in a robotics engineer first, but no one imagined there would be any problems. I must have mind-programmed half of the robots in the hospital."

Weinblatt chuckled. "Your mind-programming in a D-7 unit, the way it's been modified—just couldn't handle it. Kind of a spooky way to collect blood, you know."

The doctor scratched his chin. "I'm a little concerned. Those were my neural patterns in John's mind-program. Something in my patterns . . . just what was it that caused John to attempt suicide?"

"Doctor, it's not like you had John out shopping for groceries or shampooing a rug—the kinds of things D-7's are meant for. You had it crawling the city slums stealing blood. Your self-imprint couldn't handle it. The commands and counter commands were there, but so were a lot of other things: your feelings of guilt, morality, nightmares. I suppose you could say John died of remorse. Next time you have a touchy imprint to do, let us handle it."

Doctor Parvane raised his brows and nodded. "Do you have the artificial mind-program?"

Weinblatt reached into his tool case and withdrew a black plastic container. He opened it and removed a small red module. "This is it." He plugged it into the open chest cavity. "Doctor Heinmann back at the lab worked on this one. He said John didn't enjoy his work; but he should now." The technician activated the unit and closed the chest cover.

Doctor Parvane looked at the robot's face. "John? Can you hear me?"

The robot opened its eyes and looked at the doctor. "Yess."

Doctor Parvane frowned and looked at the technician. "John sounds different."

"Heinmann used his own voice print." Weinblatt closed his tool case and put on his coat.

The doctor looked back at the robot. "As soon as you put your clothes on, John, it's back to work."

John sat up and swung his legs from the table to the floor. "Tenk you, doktor."

The doctor and the technician left the room, closing the door behind them. John stood and dressed. When he was finished he walked to the door and opened it. A few steps into the hallway, he staggered away from a window, then fled back into the windowless laboratory.

He stood, waiting for the dark to come.

After rejecting **"Requiem for Spacemaster Jones"** once, the same editor asked to see it again—and then rejected it again. This story is a case of "almost, but not quite," and those are the ones editors hate the most because they take up the most time with nothing to show for it. A rejection is still a rejection, but it's nice to know that this story caused some worry in the process of getting rejected. The problem is a subtle one. Read and ponder away.

Spacemaster Jones grabbed the *Galactic Trotter*'s throttle, his steely blue eyes riveted to the viewplate in anticipation. Behind those eyes, he mentally calculated the twenty-four digit navigational fixes through hyperspace to the Sol System. His reflection in the viewplate grinned back at him, exposing twin rows of brilliant, even teeth set in a square, granite-carved jaw. He saw his blond crewcut standing straight and free from gray in a defiant refusal of his fifty years. Healthy, handsome, heterosexual, "And, Republican too, by God!" he whispered. Flipping on the acceleration reduction field, he jammed the throttle to the fire-wall.

"Doodle-de-doodle-eoo?" asked his faithful traveling companion and co-pilot, Thrugg, a twelve-tentacled Morfugg from the nests of Mars.

"Hah?"

"Doodle-de-doodle-eoo?" A frequency of impatience entered Thrugg's transmission.

"Thrugg, turn on your universal translator. Although I have lived as one of the Morfugg and have been taken into a nest and honored with a lifewand, I still can't make any sense out of that doodle stuff."

Thrugg screwed an object into the audio hole between his eye stalks. "I apologize, Spacemaster. The thing bothers my sinuses." Thrugg's twelve tentacles stood out straight for a moment and then relaxed, signifying a sneeze initiated and completed. "My question related to our destination. To where is the *Trotter* bound this time?" Thrugg groped behind his acceleration bed with an odd tentacle and retrieved a box of Kleenex.

"We are bound for the green hills of Earth, my friend. Terra; the blue planet. To the land of my birth; my heritage; my freedom—"

"Not Nebraska again." Thrugg's tentacles straightened, then re-laxed. He dabbed with a tissue beneath a tentacle.

"That's disgusting."

"If you think that's disgusting, Spacemaster, you should see yourself floss your teeth. Ugh!"

"You can put the used tissues into the recycler, can't you? You don't have to throw them all over the damned deck! Christ, the last time we went into freefall—"

"All right, all right, already." Thrugg slithered from his acceleration bed, picked up the used tissue with one tentacle and opened the recycler with another. Passing the tissue from tentacle to tentacle, it eventually reached the recycler. He dropped it into the compartment and closed it. He sneezed again and dabbed under the appropriate tentacle. "Why do we go to Sol III, Spacemaster?"

Spacemaster wrinkled his nose and turned back to the viewplate. "We have been away for a long time, Thrugg. It's time that we were checking in. Another adventure will be waiting for us." He watched as the star-filled viewplate wavered and then went blank. "We are into hyperspace, faithful friend. Soon we shall be in the home system."

Thrugg gathered up more used tissues and dumped them into the recycler. "I don't want to go to Earth."

"What?!" The Earthling leveled his steely blue gaze at the Martian. "Have you lost your courage, Thrugg?"

Thrugg sneezed. "Spacemaster, I have followed your exploits across nine galaxies, from the ice-covered wastes of Pergknocker to the steaming jungles of Nargafarg. I have grappled with the Bullgorthian Slime Hog and battled the Vugzornian Fang Beetle. My courage is as yours." Thrugg shrugged four tentacles. "But if I don't get in some R and R on Mars pretty soon and dry up these sinuses, I fear the condition will become permanent." He picked up a Vicks inhaler and stuck it under another tentacle. "Aaahhhh!"

At that moment the viewplate wavered again, then filled with new stars, and the brightest of these was Sol. Spacemaster sniffed back a tear.

"You want to use my inhaler?"

"Get away from me! Look there! It's Sol, the homestar. Deep within your slimy carcass are not the fibres of your race tugged by that sight?"

Thrugg aimed one of his eye stalks at the viewplate. "Oh, yeah. You see where I put my Smith Brothers Cough Drops?"

The viewplate flashed bright orange and the ship lurched violently as it came into the grip of a powerful force field. Spacemaster slapped his knee. "Tallyho, Thrugg! We won't have to wait to get to Earth for our next adventure!"

"Damn! Lost my inhaler."

As the rocking of the ship calmed, the pair detected a humming, crackling sound. Three shapes began materializing in the cockpit. The first to form was an average-sized human male garbed in a simple gray uniform and cap. The next one was taller, slender and dressed in a dark blue jumpsuit with the trouser legs tucked into mauve boots that highlighted his makeup. The third, shorter than the others, wore a strange suit that covered his entire body excepting only his face. A reddish cloak with hood adorned his shoulders. His eyes were blue from corner to corner.

"I am Paul Atredes," said blue eyes as though he expected applause. Spacemaster shrugged as Thrugg crossed his stalks to stifle a sneeze. "Perhaps you know of me as Muad'Dib, the Kwisatz Haderach?"

"Never heard of you . . . Maude, was it?"

"Muad'Dib!"

"Whatever." Spacemaster shook his head. "What's the matter with your eyes?"

The fellow in the blue jumpsuit waved a limp wrist at the Spacemaster. "Paul, let's not drag this out. We have four other ships to meet." He tossed the hair back from his eyes and smiled at Spacemaster. "I am Nicholas Bennington Flair. Paul, Officer Andrew Rusch and I form your shock committee."

"Shock . . . ?"

Flair looked around Spacemaster at Thrugg, who squatted on the deck looking for his inhaler. "I say, thing, you should be listening to this."

Thrugg's stalks, now bloodshot, turned in Flair's direction. "You god any Gleeneggs?"

Flair frowned. "What is this tongue, creature?"

"Kleenex," clarified Spacemaster. "You have any Kleenex?"

"Sorry." Thrugg went back to look for his inhaler.

"Never mind about the Kleenex, Flair. What's this all about?"

Flair checked a small clipboard strapped to his wrist. "You are Spacemaster Jones?"

"Yeah. So what?"

"Could I ask what you are doing here?"

Spacemaster snorted. "Here? This is *my* ship! What in blazes are *you* doing here?"

Flair sighed. "I meant, what are you doing here in the Sol System?"

Spacemaster's brows went up. "I gotta right! This is my home system!" He folded his arms. "Not that it's any of your business, but I am returning to be assigned a new adventure." Flair looked knowingly at his two companions, then turned back, a look of worn pity on his face.

"Perhaps you should sit down."

"I'm gonna stand right here until you three jerks tell me what this is all about!"

Flair shook his head. "Typical 1950 Syndrome." The other two nodded. "Look, Space, you've been gone a long, long time. Things have changed—"

"Changed? Changed how?"

"There will be no more adventures. Not for you."

"Nonsense!"

"Your day is over, Space. The shock committees have been formed to prepare you old mossbacks for the changes. If you can change with them, well and good. If not . . . "

Spacemaster laughed. "You little punk! In my time I've logged more miles—"

"See," said Flair to his companions. "He hasn't even gone metric." Muad'Dib snickered into his stillsuit while Officer Rusch could only shake his head. Rusch stepped forward.

"Look, Jones, the problems are different and the resolutions have changed. Hell, you can't have a throttle on an FTL drive any more. But the big change is people. We have taken over. We don't need you."

"Don't need me?" Spacemaster spat on the deck. "Alone I battled the entire empire of Zarek to save the life of Princess Rhodanerd. With my bare hands I dueled with Gorblotch, King of the Fowlzukkian Bloodsuckers—"

"Two-bit space opera," snorted Rusch.

Spacemaster looked the three over. "Well, what's so hot about you characters?"

Muad'Dib raised his hand. "Allow me, Andrew. You see, Officer Rusch is with the New York Police Department in 1999 with Earth populated past the breaking point—where survival demands more than Earth can provide. Gaunt starvation stalks the globe; suicide is encouraged to make more room; the bodies of the dead are used to feed the living." Muad'Dib bowed toward Officer Rusch who smiled in return.

Spacemaster clapped his hands together. "Great! Sounds like a terrific problem, Rusch. How'd you solve it?"

The committee chuckled. Rusch held up his hands. "I didn't, Jones. I just . . . let it go."

"Let it . . . " Spacemaster shook his head. "What about you, Flair?"

"Well, I'm a division director in a highly structured, technological society."

"What did you do? Fight it? Overthrow it and install a society of man, of the individual?"

"Actually, I got caught messing around with my boss's wife." Flair drew a finger suggestively across his throat.

"What a couple of losers." Spacemaster turned to Muad'Dib. "What about you, shorty?"

"I became the leader of the people of Arrakis, called Dune, throwing down the rule of the oppressive Harkonnens."

Spacemaster beamed. "Hey! Now, that's something I could sink my teeth in—"

"Then," continued Muad'Dib, "I led a bloody jihad across the galaxy slaying the innocent by the billions—"

Spacemaster held out his hands. "For crying out loud! Two nothings and a candidate for the laughing academy! And *you* have taken over?"

Muad'Dib nodded. "Become one of us, Spacemaster." He pulled a card from his cape pocket. "You'll need one of these."

Spacemaster looked at the card, his eyes growing wide in disbelief. "A *union* card? *Me* in a *union?*"

"We're all members."

"Fat chance!" He tossed the card back to Muad'Dib. "By the way, shorty, what *is* wrong with your eyes?"

"It is a side-effect of the geriatric spice melange. Here, try some." He held out a lid.

"You're a junkie, too?"

"C'mon. Just try a little. It's only 620,000 solaris the decagram."

"Spice my foot, you little junk dealer! Get away from me! The next thing you'll be telling me is that you're homos!"

Flair stepped forward. "As a matter of fact—"

"I don't want to hear it!" Spacemaster Jones collapsed onto his acceleration bed, his granite-carved, blue-eyed face in his hands.

Rusch shook his head. "I told you he couldn't change."

"Wad aboud me?" asked Thrugg.

Rusch studied the Morfugg. "Perhaps, but the tentacles have to go. Wouldn't you say, Flair?"

Flair nodded. "Gauche. Simply megatooty."

Spacemaster Jones moaned. "Why? Why are you doing this?"

"Things are different," answered Flair, "and 28.35 grams of prevention is worth 453.59237 grams of cure."

Thrugg slowly shook his bulb. "After thad, I guezz I'll sday wid da Spazemazder. Sure you god no Gleeneggs?"

"Terribly sorry." Flair pulled out a piece of paper and held it in front of Jones. "Sign that. It shows that we informed you of the union requirements before you returned to Earth."

Tears dribbled down Spacemaster's cheeks as he raised his head. "Go to hell. I'm not signing anything."

"Sign it!" commanded Maud'Dib, using The Voice. A Papermate leaped from Spacemaster's pocket and unseen forces made his hand grab the pen and move it across the paper. As the three assumed their positions and dematerialized, Spacemaster bawled. Thrugg sneezed.

Later, alone on the bridge, Thrugg guided the *Galactic Trotter* back into deep space. They could have gone back to Earth, except Spacemaster could not face it—the new Earth. Spacemaster had disappeared into his cabin and had remained there since leaving the Sol System. As he rubbed Vicks Vaporub into his carapace, Thrugg was very sad.

"Thrugg! Thrugg!" The Martian heard the cry coming from below deck, followed by the clatter of running boots. Spacemaster Jones leaped through the hatch and landed on the bridge. "Quick! Turn around, Thrugg! We're going back!"

"Wad's ub, Spazemazder?"

"Look!" He shoved a paperback book into Thrugg's tentacles. "They need us down there. Those characters were trying to eliminate the competition!"

Thrugg leafed through the book and pointed one stalked eye at Spacemaster Jones. "*Star Wars?*"

"That's it, Thrugg! A princess in distress, an evil lord, interplanetary revolution, a mere boy destroying an oppressive empire—it's *beautiful!*"

Thrugg made the necessary adjustments and turned the ship. In seconds he read the book and nodded his bulb at Spacemaster. "Id iz az you say, Spazemazder. We are saved. Juzd one small problem."

"What's that, Thrugg?"

"Where'd da book cub frub? Da committee didn'd brig id."

Spacemaster shrugged. "If *Star Wars* isn't worried about little details like that, why should we?"

Introduction:
Here, with **"Then Darkness Again,"** we have a twist on a problem covered in an earlier story. A hint: Upon completing this piece, what are the first two words that pop into your mind?

"This is the Big Dip on two-two-one point three. Anybody got their audios on out there." Al Bragg released his mike key while the twenty seconds ticked off. More than a twenty-second lag between transmissions was a drag. Al checked his instruments and the screen depicting his place in relation to the galactic arm . . . eighteen, nineteen, twenty.

Al adjusted the frequency and thumbed his mike. "This is the Big Dip on two-two-one point four. Looking for chat-chat; anybody there?" Al looked at his screen and tried to pick out the Sol system by eye. The computer could have given him an automatic fix, but then that would give Al less to do; and Al was bored, not to mention homesick . . . eighteen, nineteen, twenty.

"This is the Big Dip on two-two-one point five craving some communication." Al sighed, wishing he hadn't cut across the void from the center to the arm. *Nobody ever goes this way. Three standard weeks from the candy bar quadrants and I haven't raised a peep* . . . eighteen, nineteen, twenty. *Bet the translator's on the poopers again.*

"Biggy Dippy on two-two-one point six looking for some tricks; let's hear it out there." *Well, it was either go this way or go the long way around empty. Nuts. I could have found a load. Guess I just wanted to get home* . . . eighteen, nineteen, twenty.

"This is the Dipper on two-two-one point seven searching heaven for some talk-talk."

LADLE, THIS BEAR.

Al jumped, then smiled. Someone out there, and the literal translations were half the fun of chatter—and the game. "Bear, this is the Dipper. I haven't raised a soul for a sun's age. Where are you headed?"

ON TOP, LADEL. ONLY ONE. AND YOU?

"Negative, Big Bear. What is your destination?"

I SORRY. THE CENTER. QUADRANT TWENTY AND FIVE. WANT THE GAME TO PLAY?

"You bet."

THAT AFFIRMATIVE? NO IS WAGER?

"Affirmative. Shall you start, or shall I?"

START.

"Hey, Big Bear, the translator's not up to combined or absent personal pronouns. You or me?"

YOU.

"Okay." Al rubbed his chin. The trick was to be truthful without giving away the location. "My planet is beautiful."

MY PLANET IS UGLY.

Al frowned. *Hell, I've gabbed with aliens from hunks of black ice that thought their own planets were beautiful while Earth was 'ugly.'* "Okay, Big Bear. The atmosphere is blue with white clouds of water vapor. It rains, making the surface rich with vegetation."

SKY BLUE A LITTLE. YELLOW FROM DUST AND FEW CLOUDS. THE GROUND IS HARD AND DRY. RAINS LITTLE; GROWS LESS.

Al pursed his lips, then shook his head. "I can't get it, Big Bear. You?"

NO.

"Want to try government?" Al smiled, hoping the Bear would fall for it. Populated desert planets—maybe twenty of them—and Al knew them all. A few hints on governmental structure would be all that was needed.

IS GOOD. ME FIRST?

"Go."

PEOPLE MINE . . . ARE OPPRESSED. ALWAYS. OUR GOVERN-MENT OR OTHERS, NO DIFFERENCE IT MAKES. WE HAD REV-OLUTIONS. MANY, BUT NO DIFFERENCE IT MAKES.

Al scratched his head, trying to think of a dustball in political turmoil. *Might be Garnetsid . . . but, no; the Bear said he has only one head.* He keyed his mike. "Long ago, we had a revolution. But we are free. The wars are all behind us. We can pretty much choose what we want to be, and we're well off. Wealthy. I own my own ship."

AH! IS GOOD. I GUESS NOW. MINTAKA TWELVE?

"Negative, Big Bear. I'll go first with economy. I said we were wealthy. I bet we're the financial center of our quadrant."

NOT IS MINTAKA TWELVE?

"Negative on Mintaka Twelve." Al chuckled. He'd caught several drivers on Mintaka Twelve.

NO UNDERSTAND. THIS GOOD. MY BEINGS ARE POOR ON PLANET MINE. FOR REASON, GO TO QUADRANT TWENTY AND FIVE BUY WEAPONS NOW. YOU GUESS LADLE NOW?

Al slapped his knee. "It has to be Sadr Five, Big Bear. Right?"

NEGATIVE, LADLE. GUESS ANOTHER TIME?

Al frowned at the static in the transmission. "I'm out of guesses, Big Bear. Say, how do you read?"

EYES. TWO.

Al sighed. "Your reception. Is it getting weak?"

FOUR AND SOME, LADLE.

"I guess this is it. You give up?

YOU?

"Affirmative, Big Bear. I don't get stumped very often. What's your planet?"

EARTH. THIRD IN SYSTEM OF SOL.

"That can't . . . Big Bear, go off translator and retransmit." Al frowned at his speaker.

TIERRA.

"Are you . . . Spanish?"

MEJECANO . . . HABLA INGLES! POR QUE?

"I'm from Earth. North America."

GRINGO?

"Yeah, wetback. I guess it's how you look at it."

SI.

"Small galaxy, isn't it?"

ES VERDAD . . . ADIOS.

"Yeah . . . good-bye, Big Bear." Al shrugged and adjusted the frequency. "This is the Big Dip on two-two-one point eight . . . ."

Introduction:

This item, **"The Gift,"** was inflicted upon Stanley Schmidt only sparse weeks after his investiture as the new editor of *Analog*. Stanley's raspberry was very kind. "The Gift" is a letter story, and simple diagramming will show you what's wrong with it.

To: Haagraak Mus Ugoch,
   Chief Librarian, Milky Way Galactic Library
   Pinwat Library Station,
   32nd Quadrant, 17.321.4

From: Ampus D. Grampus, Secretary
   United Quadrants Commission on Underdeveloped Planets
   26th Quadrant, 773.486.21

My dear Mister Ugoch:

1. Please be advised that the UQ Commission on Underdeveloped Planets is most pleased with the Library's speedy compliance with Assembly Resolution A-227,398, "Resolution In Support Of The Dissemination Of Library Relics," subsequent to the complete computerization of the Library's vast collection. We have already received notices from several planetary governments gratefully acknowledging receipt of their rare volumes.

2. The Commission would also commend the Library for the definition of "habitable" it used in choosing the number of volumes to send to each planet, although that particular definition reduced the number of volumes sent to each *inhabited* planet to three. It shows the proper spirit. However, the Commissioners have asked me to bring several things to your attention:

A. The inhabitants of Letlite IV tend toward literalness, despite having neither a science nor literature of their own. Hence, the Commissioners feel that the choice of *Origin of Species, The Old Testament,* and *The Chariots of the Gods* was a poor one. Since the three factions exterminated themselves attempting to settle the issue, no remedial action is suggested.

B. The selection of *The Joy of Sex, Fanny Hill,* and *The Life of the Marquis de Sade* for the hermaphroditic culture of Swassi II could have had terrible consequences, but fortunately they are merely confused. The commission asks if something more suitable could be submitted, such as old scripts from *Gilligan's Island* or *Battlestar Galactica*?

C. We have yet to learn the full consequences of delivering *Stranger In a Strange Land, The Joy of Cooking,* and *The Voyages of Captain Cook* to the carnivores on Velbaad III, since we are still awaiting word from the Commission representative. We fear the worst. A good, old-fashioned dose of Terran 20th Century vegetarianism would seem to be indicated. The Commission bows to your judgment in the selection of appropriate texts.

D. *The Feminine Mystique* and *The Baby Trap* found an eager audience in the sexually oppressed population of Naag VII, but the poor henpecked males lost interest after reading *An Introduction To Biology*. However, the female masters of Naag VII saw the writing on the wall (in the volumes you selected, actually) and completely exterminated the male population. Their representative to the UQ has placed an urgent request for something on cloning. *Very* urgent.

E. I realize that the distribution of volumes was determined through a random computer program; however, several of the Commissioners find the selection of *Oedipus Rex,* Freud's *The Sexual Enlightenment Of Children,* and *Portnoy's Complaint* for the Rutfiends of Jakula VI something more than a coincidence. Twice, delegations of Rutfiend matrons have appealed to the Commission for relief. I do not know what to suggest; something on jogging, perhaps?

The list is virtually endless. Despite the limited success of the program, the Commission wishes you to be advised that "An Act To Save Our Galaxy" was passed unanimously by the UQ Assembly. The act halts the further distribution of library books, and requires the Library to recall—where possible—those volumes already distributed. Exceptions for remedial action have been provided for in the text.

Sincerely yours,
Ampus D. Grampus,
Secretary

Introduction:
This tale, **"What Would Harry Do?"**—even after a rewrite—wrinkled brows at both *IA'sfm* and *Analog*. This is a *very* subtle problem, and one that can possibly be corrected. I have suggested one such correction in the critique for this story. See if you can tell what the problem is, then devise a solution.

Willis E. Rockwell, President of the United States of America, held up his **The Buck Stops Here** replica and faced it toward Prewitt Davies, special assistant to the President. Rockwell tapped the replica with a well-manicured finger. "The secret in making this sign work, Prewitt, is to organize things in such a manner that the buck never shows up here in the first place." Rockwell replaced the sign and squared it with the edge of the desk facing toward the ornate marble fireplace opposite his vantage point in the Oval Office. "I didn't get where I am today by letting subordinates pass on their petty decisions for me to make. Responsibility, Prewitt! I don't want anyone working for me who is afraid to make a decision. Understood?"

"Yes, Mr. President—"

"I'm leaving for Camp David in an hour, then I'm taking a few days off for golf in Augusta. I deserve this vacation, Prewitt, and I have every intention of taking it. Now, is this problem of such a pressing nature that it can't wait for a couple of weeks?"

"I believe so, Mr. President. Walt Tubbman felt that it was very serious; Jane and Milt feel the same way—"

"What could this problem be that it stumps my secretaries of defense, state and intelligence?"

"It has to do with Project Aeolus. NASA Director, Nancy Crown, said—"

"Prewitt, how many do you have out there?"

Prewitt sighed. "Besides those already mentioned, there's Brubaker and Ozawa from State. They hold down the Russian affairs and space relations desks. Then General Cushing, Chairperson of the Joint—"

"A number, Prewitt. How many?"

"Sixteen, Mr. President."

Rockwell shook his head, then leaned forward and tapped his sign. "Every person in this administration, from the lowliest clerk to the Vice-President, is supposed to have one of these." The President frowned. "This particular buck seems to have logged a lot of mileage before it stopped at my door."

"Mr. President, no one has been shirking responsibility, I assure you. The problem is simply far beyond their area of decision. Project Aeolus—"

Rockwell held up his hand. "I don't want to hear this cabbage chewed twice, Prewitt. Can you state this problem yourself?"

Prewitt Davies shifted his weight from his right foot to his left foot. "I'd rather that you listened to the others. I am confused about several areas, and the implications—"

"Very well." Rockwell looked at his watch and shook his head. "I want you to go out there and high-grade that bunch of buck-passers. I want two people who can state the problem, and be brief in doing so."

"Yes, Mr. President." Davies walked briskly to the door to the left of the fireplace, opened it and closed it softly behind him. Only a moment later, the door opened and Davies ushered in two men. "Mr. President, the Secretary of State and Doctor Thornhill, Director of Project Aeolus."

Rockwell nodded at the two men. Thornhill, a graying wisp of humanity in an ill-fitting suit, stood fidgeting with his frightened eyes darting back and forth behind thick glasses. Milton Weissburger, Secretary of State, his usually immaculate pinstripes looking as though he had slept in them, nodded back. "Well, Milt, what's this all about?"

The Secretary looked at Davies, then cocked his head in Doctor Thornhill's direction. "I think Dr. Thornhill should begin."

Rockwell turned to Thornhill and saw that the little man was frightened to distraction. The President smiled and displayed the even, gleaming dentures that were worth fifteen percent of the vote any November. The doctor seemed more startled than assured, and the President replaced his smile with an expression of cultured bland nonhostility. "Doctor?"

"Yes . . . yes, Mister President. I am the director of the project—Project Aeolus." Thornhill swallowed, then turned toward Davies. "Doctor

Bellinger should be the one explaining this. I'm an administrator."
Rockwell sat motionless and Davies averted his glance. Thornhill
turned to the President and held out his hands. "It's an outgrowth of
Bellinger's work in matter transmission. That . . . involves the con-
version of mass to transportable energy, then the reconversion of that
energy into a form resembling the original mass, but in a different
location." He licked his lips. "We—NASA—were applying Bellinger's
theories to interstellar and intergalactic travel. The Bellinger effect,
you know?" Rockwell shook his head.

"No."

Thornhill wiped a palm across his face. "Well, the experiments involved a transmitter and receiver. An object placed into the transmitter
would be materialized in the receiver. But, you can see how this would
limit space travel, since before you could use the system, it would be
necessary to ship a receiver there first, and at sub-light speed it would
take countless years—"

"I get the drift, Doctor." Rockwell glanced at his watch. "Continue."

Thornhill nodded and pulled at his collar. "Well, Bellinger worked
on a way to take a receiver and transmit it ahead of the object to be
transmitted. He found that with the receiver at rest, it could be pro-
jected forward a fraction of a millimeter. Those were his earlier experiments. But the projection increased dramatically with an object
in motion. Also, he found that with each subsequent transmission-
reception cycle, each subsequent projection was increased by a factor
of five."

Thornhill again wiped his face, glanced at Davies, then looked back
at the President. "Sir, Aeolus was our first attempt at applying Bellinger's work to actual space travel. The *U.S.S. Alaska* was loaned to
us by Defense and fitted with the necessary equipment. Please believe
we made every effort to protect the crew!"

Rockwell heaved a sigh. "Please continue, Doctor."

"It was the loss of mass per cycle detected by Bellinger in his early
experiments. It wasn't important for a few cycles, but we determined
that it would be dangerous for large numbers of cycles, depending on
what part of the mass was lost, you see?"

Rockwell nodded. "Get on with it, Thornhill."

"Yessir. Well, Bellinger devised a means of tapping the area sur-
rounding the ship at any given point for convertible material to make
up the loss. Well . . . we tried it out. Something went wrong."

"Wrong?"

Thornhill nodded. "We don't know what. Bellinger theorizes that
space has partially reflective zones that the MT beam went through.
Somehow . . . well, after the preprogrammed number of cycles were
completed, we had two *Alaska*'s instead of one!"

Rockwell rubbed his chin. "Now, let me understand. There are now
two ships—two identical ships called *U.S.S. Alaska?*"

Thornhill nodded. "Two ships, two Captain O'Malleys, two crews,
each the spitting image of the other."

Rockwell scratched the back of his neck. "Interesting. Very interesting, Doctor. But why bring this to me? Experiments have failed before."

Milton Weissburger put a hand on Thornhill's shoulder. "Perhaps I should take it from here, Mr. President?"

"Okay, Milt."

"Sir, the first problem is that we now have two *Alaska*'s instead of one."

Rockwell shook his head. "Whenever you see a problem, Milt, look for the opportunities it presents. It looks to me as though we just got ourselves six billion bucks' worth of battleship for next to nothing. That doesn't even consider the cost of manning it with an experienced crew."

The Secretary of State shook his head. "Sir, the additional battleship puts us in violation of the Arms Stabilization Agreement with the Soviets. The additional crew makes us overstrength. The Russians don't know about it yet, but their inspection teams can't miss something as big as a battleship forever."

Rockwell shrugged. "Why is this being brought to my office? Decommission one of the ships and discharge one of the crews."

Weissburger held out his hands. "Which one, Mr. President?" The Secretary held up a hand as the President opened his mouth to reply. "But, we can always flip a coin." Rockwell nodded. "But Walt looked into the problem, and we can't decommission one without decommissioning both. There is only one on record. The same goes for the crews. We can't fire one of them without, first, hiring them, and as soon as we do, the Soviet inspection teams will pick it up in the records—"

Rockwell shook his head and waved his arms. "Dammit, Milt! Can't my cabinet display a little initiative? This is nothing but a red tape knot. Cut through it. Fake it if you have to, but don't pass the buck to me. Read that sign on your desk sometime." Rockwell glanced at his watch. "Was there anything else?"

Weissburger pressed his hands against his temples. "The two crews, Mister President. There aren't enough wives, husbands, families and sweethearts to go around. Whichever crew gets back first will claim to be the real thing, which makes that number two crew—"

"I get the picture."

"—two thousand trained fighters cut loose on society against another two thousand trained fighters in the name of love and the sanctity of the home—"

"I *said* I get the picture. Let the Attorney General handle that. If he has to, he can clap both crews in irons until this thing gets sorted out." Rockwell turned toward Thornhill. "Doctor, is there any way to tell which crew is the original and which is the copy?"

Thornhill shrugged. "Both came from the same parent signal; they're both originals."

Rockwell wiped a bead of sweat from his upper lip. "Still, gentlemen, we are talking petty detail. I am not pleased with this day's performance. All of this could have been handled in the outer office." He raised his eyebrows. "If there is nothing else?"

Weissburger looked at Thornhill. The doctor's shoulders slumped as though his sleeves were lined with lead. "There is one . . . other thing, Mister President."

Rockwell folded his arms. "Well?"

"It has to do with the conservation of mass and energy. That extra battleship wasn't made up out of nothing. It had to come from somewhere. The mass replacement device picked up energy—and some mass that it converted to energy—" Thornhill began looking wild-eyed. "—The device was designed to pick up anything that could be used: stray hydrogen molecules, sun and starlight, dust, kinetic energy in its motion relative to stable space." Thornhill took two deep breaths. "Mr. President, it picked up a form of energy we know nothing about, but the amounts of this unknown form of energy needed to replace just a single atom at light speed measures into the tons—"

Rockwell developed a sour expression. "Thornhill, this is a problem for scientists. Fix it."

Thornhill swayed for a moment. "We can. In the future. A governor limiting the amount of energy the system is allowed to absorb." Thornhill shook his head. "But that doesn't matter. To make up that extra ship at light speeds . . . we're left with what we're calling an energy vacuum. It's like pulling a bucket of water out of a swimming pool. The remaining water rushes in to fill the empty place. That's what's happening right now in a straight track running from here—or from Earth's position three weeks ago—on past the orbit of Pluto!"

Rockwell swallowed. "Make yourself clear, Thornhill."

"Mr. President, anything that comes near that vacuum is absorbed and converted back into that unknown energy. Starlight can't even pass through it. Astronomers are looking at the track end-on right now, but in a couple of months it will be a black streak across the sky. Three months after that, Earth will be behind the vacuum in relation to the Sun for close to three weeks. Imagine no heat—no light for three weeks!"

Rockwell cleared his throat. "Go on."

Thornhill waved his arms about. "Several asteroids visible from Earth are already missing, but the vacuum is beginning to suck on Mars! We can't see it now, because of the dust storms, but our stations on Mars confirm that several landmarks have simply disappeared leaving huge, tear-shaped holes in the surface. Mars is several thousand kilometers from the vacuum. It must send out streamers in search of matter. Maybe, when the end of the streamer is satisfied, it breaks off, only making a hole." Thornhill leaned against the Secretary of State. "Mr. President, it's only a matter of weeks before it sucks up the entire planet of Mars."

Rockwell stared at his desk blotter. "Have you begun evacuating the Mars crews?"

Thornhill nodded. "Yes. But in less than a year, Earth will be in the same position. Whatinthehell are we going to do about it? My people are working on it night and day, but we don't even know what questions to ask. Right now it looks like there isn't enough material in the entire solar system to feed that damned thing . . . ."

Rockwell looked up and saw Weissburger supporting the doctor. The Aeolus Director wept as he was led out of the door. Prewitt Davies closed the door behind them, then turned to face the President. Rockwell rubbed his eyes. "Prewitt, go out but stay close to the phone. Keep all those people out there on a short leash."

"Yes, Mr. President."

The door closed and Willis E. Rockwell let out his breath. He leaned forward and turned his **The Buck Stops Here** sign around and pulled it close. *What would Harry do? What would any of them do? What could they do?* The President picked up the sign in his left hand and studied the glossy walnut grain. With his right hand he picked up one of his telephone receivers. "Prewitt?" The Presidential toe pulled out the Presidential wastebasket out from under the Presidential desk. The sign clanged as it hit the bottom. "Arrange for me to address the General Assembly of the United Nations at the earliest possible opportunity." *Why not? It's about time those do-nothings on the East River earned their keep. Let them handle it.* He kicked the wastebasket back under his desk.

CRITIQUES

"On Hold"

If you were able to diagram this piece, somewhere there is a medal waiting for you. Where is this thing taking place? Than and Dzmi are hungry, but they are not terribly concerned about finding food. What is their goal? What is the obstacle to that goal? Is that goal compelling enough around which to construct a main conflict? If it is, what is the main conflict? What are they as far as characters? What do they look like; what do they feel; what do they think? Who cares?

Here we have a two hundred word piece with two shifts in viewpoint. Who is the reader supposed to identify with? In the second scene, where is the action taking place: in the shrink's office or in a telephone booth?

What is the purpose of this story? Grope around all you want, but the purpose was this: the author was irritated at the expression "hold that thought." Whatever else such a motivation is, it is too trivial for a story.

What if thoughts could be held? What if, in some other dimension, the things we forget are food for others? "Thought for food" leaps to mind, but this is the single thing not wrong with the story. If such a dimension existed and functioned in such a manner, the story would be "science fiction."

Everything else with the story is wrong. Too many things are lacking for a proper story situation; the "aliens" are cute as the dickens; the buildup (scene #2) is almost incoherent; the resolution resolves nothing important. The story is murky, incoherent, not convincing, cutesy, trivial, and a waste of good paper and postage.

Given that there were a dimension where beings existed that fed on thoughts from our dimension, the premise for a delightfully spooky story could be made. But it would take a much longer treatment than "On Hold," and a much different treatment.

Just to add insult to injury, one of the characters is named "Than." Can you see the problem with that? I could just as well have named it "This" or "So Forth" to maximize reader confusion.

"Dry Run"

"Not convincing" is the first problem with this piece. The reader can figure out that occupational clones exist under oppressive conditions, and that the Zorik aliens have joined with the clones in a strike toward overthrowing the oppressors. But where did the aliens come from? Why did they, and why are they helping the clones? Without properly developing the characters of the Zoriks, their ability to assume the shape of teeth seems terribly handy. Perhaps this could have been cured through proper plants—perhaps not. I can't think of an environment that would evolve such a lifeform. However, the really big problem with this piece is that it is not a story. As bad as it is, it sets up a story situation, but it does not follow through with a buildup and resolution of the main conflict.

"Please Give"

I wanted to try my hand at a vampire robot. Why I wanted this is a problem between me and my shrink; the way I went about it, however, illustrates one of the dangers of letting the story drag the writer. I invented my robot, then turned him loose on the page. John found a very familiar path (ever hear the one about the robot that thought it was human? And the other one; and the other one; and . . .). Not only has this "idea" been done to death, because of that fact the ending is very predictable. The "Catch-22" is, if the ending were not predictable, the story would then be a "tomato surprise."

An additional problem: here we have a 2,000 word piece with a viewpoint shift in it that shatters reader identification. To wind it up, the title (borrowed from a bloodmobile sticker) stinks.

Too bad about this one, because I sort of liked old John.

"Requiem For Spacemaster Jones"

The market for science-fiction satire is *very* limited. In addition, there is a very thin line between well-done satire and outright slapstick comedy. There is *no* market for SF slapstick, and this piece made it across the line. The market for SF "in-jokes" is limited, but it depends on the particular jokes—they have to be funny whether the reader understands them or not.

At the time this piece was submitted, there was only one magazine editor seriously considering science fiction humor (George Scithers), and while he was pondering my piece, he was also considering "Bat Durston, Space Marshal" by G. Richard Bozarth. Both stories satirized the traditional 1950 space opera stereotype, but Bozarth did a better job of it. Besides, as George Scithers pointed out in his second rejection letter: "Do you *really* want a snarling mob of *Dune* freaks angry at you for the misappropriation of Muad'Dib? Imagine—Farmington, Maine gone, with only the great track of a colossal worm to mark its passage . . . "

"Then Darkness Again"

If the first two words that popped into your mind after reading "Darkness" were "So what?" or "Big deal" you already know what's wrong with this piece. In this story the idea appears trivial. What change did the big realization make in Al? "Al shrugged and adjusted the frequency." Any reader would do the same.

The reason this is a twist on the problem of trying to construct a story around a trivial idea is because what I did was to take a very important idea and make it trivial because of the story I constructed around it. What we are, how we see things, how we see ourselves in the scheme of things, and communicating this to other beings (human or alien) through this poor thing we call "language," is probably the most important problem that exists. But, "Al shrugged . . . "

The thing to learn from "Then Darkness Again," is not to start a story with the first thing that pops into your head. Do not begin too soon. Examine ideas, story situations, characters, etc., the same way a diamond cutter examines rough stones prior to cutting and faceting. A diamond cutter who simply picked up stones and whacked at them with a sledgehammer would probably be shot; storytellers who take ideas and whack at them with the first things that come to mind get rejections.

"The Gift"

As Stanley Schmidt pointed out, a bunch of good one-liners do not a story make. Diagramming tells the tale. A story situation has been set up, establishing a main conflict; but there it stops. No buildup; no resolution; no story; no sale.

"What Would Harry Do?"

To cause President Rockwell to ditch his **The Buck Stops Here** sign into the trash can, I handed him a buck that just wouldn't stop. In its present structure, the story would have been acceptable had I handed Rockwell a somewhat smaller problem. Much brow wrinkling at *IA'sfm* and *Analog* eventually produced the answer: The story is complete, and resolves. However, the problem that causes Rockwell to dump his sign is of such magnitude and possible interest, that the readers would be left feeling cheated without finding out what happens after that—how is the *big* problem going to turn out?

The solution to repairing this tale is to resolve the biggie problem. However, if Rockwell solves it, it ruins the gag at the end. If he doesn't solve it (with a solution tacked onto the end), the gag gets lost in the middle. There are a number of ways to salvage this tale. One that appeals to me is to make the following changes: First, change the viewpoint character from Rockwell to Prewitt Davies; second, run the story as is, with Davies catching a glimpse of Rockwell dumping his sign just before he orders his assistant to arrange the UN address. Davies smiles and dumps his own **The Buck Stops Here** sign, then makes the arrangements.

Scene break and viewpoint shift. We're in the Captain's cabin on one of the

*U.S.S. Alaska*s. Captain O'Malley is literally beside himself, trying to figure out what to do as, with each passing day, the problem worsens while the UN flounders around. The scene between the two Captains O'Malley could be wrung for many laughs. During the scene, the plants to solve the problem would be laid. The plants needed are: the establishment of Bellinger (two of them, actually) being on board(s), and the scientist(s)' occupation(s) with trying to reverse the process.

Meanwhile, back at the White House, Prewitt Davies is trying to hold the hounds at bay. High-ranking officials, press, pressure groups, Congressbeings, foreign heads of state—everybody is in a panic. Phone call. The UN General Assembly has finally taken some action: The body has passed a resolution to entertain a motion to endorse in principle the establishment of a committee charged with formulating the language acceptable to a majority of the Assembly to be engrossed in the formal motion to table the issue. In other words, the buck has been passed to that great legislative filebox in the sky.

Time passes. President Rockwell is surrounded by telephones waiting for one of them to come forth with a straw of hope. Prewitt Davies removes an empty whiskey bottle from the President's desk and heads for the door as one of the phones rings. Rockwell pushes the conference listening button (enabling both him and Davies to hear the caller). It's Doctor Thornhill, Project Aeolus Director. Bellinger and the formerly two Captains O'Malley have worked it out and have reversed the process! A new planet was formed from the leftover mass dumped as the two ships became one, but it is in a stable orbit between Earth and Mars. The threat is over!

Davies rushes to the door to call for a press conference, shouts his instructions through the open door, then turns back to see Rockwell removing a familiar sign from his desk drawer. He places **The Buck Stops Here** sign on his desk and squares it with the desk's edge. "Do you understand now, Prewitt? This matter could have been handled at a lower level all the time." He taps the sign. "I want one of these on everyone's desk, from the lowliest clerk . . . "

CHAPTER EIGHT

WHERE TO START: A METHOD

Just prior to writing this chapter, I attended a science-fiction convention where the subject of story starting points was tackled. Panelist George H. Scithers asked the different writers in the audience where they began in writing a story. Before that session, I was convinced that I always began with a character or characters; but by the time I was asked, I remembered a story I had done that began with an environmental premise. After the session, I thought of another story that began with a biological premise, and an entire series that began with nothing more than an image of a desert night scene. One story began with just a feeling of rage. I had to go home and search through all of my files to try and find a story in which I *had* begun with a character. In my files, I found something curious: I seldom start a story with any single thing. Almost every story I have written has a genealogy of seemingly unrelated ideas and details.

I was startled at some of the seemingly trivial things that served as my starting points for stories. And as I examined my story notes, the unconscious method I used to build stories from a multitude of those starting points became apparent. This was the fourth time—in connection with writing projects—that I tracked down all of the things that went into writing a particular story. Each time I found that I used the same method. I am always keeping notes on any and all ideas. The notes may or may not be written with a particular story in mind. Nevertheless, when they don't seem to go anywhere, they get tossed into my story dump. Sometime later I will get an "idea" in combination with a strong urge to write a story. When I am writing, it is all in my head, and it appeared to me that all I was doing was creating a character and letting it run around on the paper.

The truth, however, is that almost every aspect of the story has been worked out in advance, often in great detail. The urge to write comes when those bits and pieces of story parts come together in my subconscious like some kind of great puzzle. But in comparing the finished story with its parent ideas, I found that most of the ideas had been altered. Between the last of the note-taking and the start of the writing, therefore, is what I call a "stewing period" during which the ideas are subconsciously shaped and assembled. This chapter presents the genealogy of one such story, beginning with the notes, following with the "stewing period," then the actual writing.

STARTING POINTS & INITIAL DEVELOPMENT

Since I don't date notes, I have no idea in what order the following notes were made. They were developed in spastic concurrency over a period of about four months. In addition, many of my notes are one-word memory triggers that would make no sense to anyone. I have, therefore, written them out in an attempt at coherency. On the other hand, several of these files contained story starts that ran up to ten thousand words. These have been presented only in outline.

FILE #1

Starting Point:

Begin a story in English, dropping in alien language words and phrases along the way, until the reader is sufficiently familiar with the alien language that the last paragraph of the story can be written entirely in the alien tongue.

Initial Development:

1. The first step is to invent the alien language. It has to be alien, but still easily learned if the reader is going to be able to make it through the last paragraph without a fight. [I worked up the grammar, spelling, pronunciation, and a vocabulary of about three hundred words. The end result was a cross between Spanish, Japanese, Hebrew, and Piglatin.]

2. Invent a situation that would justify the language exercise. One character must learn the language from another, or at least the reader has to learn it.

General semantics teaches that certain terms (called semantic blanks) are regarded as representing some aspect of reality (have meaning) but, instead, are meaningless (have no corresponding referent in reality); "justice," "fair," "socialism," "reasonable," and "rights" being among the many. The theory is that if two persons, each speaking a different language and understanding none of the other's language, and each one refusing to learn the other's language, invented a third language for purposes of communication, they would not be able to talk about "justice," or "socialism."

One can point at a rock and call it a "blug." The second person agrees, and from then on when the word "blug" is used, each party will know what is being referred to. But what do you point at to arrive at an agreement on a term for "justice"?

3. What if negotiators representing different political powers (human and alien) were cut off from any means of translating their words and had to invent a language of their own? Why invent a language of their own? They could sit out the technical difficulty and continue as before unless the difficulty were one that, first, caused an immediate danger, and second, could not be cured in time. Put them in space. The negotiators must be separated from the translators (either mechanical or human) for some credible reason.

Let's say that all sides to this negotiation are highly suspicious of each other, and that the ground rules limit just the chiefs of each negotiating team into a self-contained vessel—such as a shuttle. The translators (human and alien) do their work by remote means from the parent ship. Slam! Sabotage. The parent ship explodes, blowing the shuttle clear. The tiny craft with its limited range and supplies is stranded in space. The only ones aboard are the negotiation team chiefs: three different kinds of aliens and an English-speaking human. They must work together to have a chance at surviving, but before that, they must be able to communicate. They begin trying.

4. Now, to back up some and stick in some characters. First, the human negotiator. The experience is going to have to teach him something, so make him a hidebound, ding-word happy diplomatic type. What is he going to learn? The brotherhood of creatures, we're in this all together, stuff is too old. What about the theory itself? Ninety-nine percent of all religions, codes of ethics, ideologies, moralities, concepts of right and wrong are founded on ding-words; semantic blanks; if it doesn't have an existing-in-reality, mutually agreed upon referent, the term is meaningless. That would be something to learn.

5. How is our diplomat going to get the lesson along with the reader? The premise of semantic blanks must be explained. Another character: the human negotiator's translator. A cynical fellow who has spent his life studying languages, and seeing them used and abused through negotiations of various kinds. The diplomat and the translator are having a talk prior to the negotiators boarding the shuttle. The diplomat makes campaign noises about "serving the good of humanity," and the translator tells him he's full of bull, then why. Diplomat disagrees, then boards shuttle.

6. What are these characters negotiating about? The first round opens making clear to the reader what the issue is. A territorial thing: war, economics—something like that—replete with fine, high-sounding phrases signifying nothing. It has to be done in English, and the human diplomat is the only one getting the conversation in English. Diplomat is viewpoint character.

6. Blam! The parent ship goes up, the shuttle is blown clear, and our cast is stranded without a common word between them. Now what? They are diplomats—not pulp SF geniuses who can take bobby pins and wads of bubble gum and rig a faster-than-light drive or universal translator. They are all word mechanics—ding-word mechanics at that. They hate each other's guts. The long arm of coincidence rule prevents the Seventh Cavalry from riding in and saving them; they have to work their own way out. First, a little trust. Then they begin pointing at various things and naming them. Just to develop a get-along-in-this-situation working language will take endless pages—particularly if the reader must learn the language as well. Working up to a "Hey-I'm-a-former-physicist-and-we-can-try-this" language level will take volumes. Ending of story? They talk each other to death.

7. Consign notes to story dump and work on something else.

FILE #2

Starting Point:

What if long-haul spaceship pilots gummed away on the radio the way CB freaks do now? It's done through a very literal translating system. Two humans—one Spanish-speaking, the other English-speaking—have their "ears on," but because of the differences in grammar and the literal translations, each one thinks he is talking to a nonhuman.

Initial Development:

1. Okay, we are writing for a primarily English-speaking audience, the English-speaking human is the viewpoint character. Along with our viewpoint character, we will let the reader think that the other guy is an alien.

2. What do they talk about? Invent "The Game." They kill time by describing their native planets to each other, each trying to be first at guessing the other's planet.

3. At last they both give up, name their home planet (Earth), then are amazed at the different perceptions they each have of the old sod. Write up story and send off [see "Then Darkness Again" in Chapter Eight, "Fatal Flaws."].

4. Story rejected. Consign to story dump.

FILE #3

Starting Point:

A vague image of a human bending over an alien. The alien is dead? Dying? It's at night in the rain. The alien elicits a promise from the human. What promise?

Initial Development:

1. Nothing there. Make not and consign to story dump.

FILE #4

Starting Point:

After reading Alex Haley's *Roots*, contemplating the African griots—men whose job it is to memorize and recite village history; the events that transpire within their lifetimes, in addition to the histories passed down to them by former griots. An amazing feat of memory; hundreds of years filed away: births, deaths, marriages, wars, visits from strangers, who went where when. Jean [my wife] is interested in genealogy and it never fails to astound me how much she knows about my family that I don't. The meaning of *Roots*: knowledge of one's lineage maintaining a strong sense of family and personal identity within a culture designed to disintegrate families and strip identities. I never had a real family of my own.

Initial Development:

1. An alien culture—vague—a lesson yard; young aliens reciting their family lines. One of the aliens must memorize much more than the rest: a thousand generations? Technologically advanced culture, so why the memorizing? African griots exist only a little because of tradition, mostly because of primitive conditions and illiteracy.

2. Having memorized the family line *is* identity in this culture; a rite of adulthood entrenched by law, custom, and tradition. Why does the one youngster have so much more to memorize than the others? Wouldn't they all have about the same number of generations to memorize? Not if there were "line founders." A specific point at which a line was founded—begun. How?

3. Memorizing an entire family tree back only a few generations—given dual parents, uncles, aunts, cousins, children, grandchildren, etc.—is a considerable tangle of relationships and number of histories to commit to memory. Given

that method of reproduction, everyone would have the same number of generations to memorize. In addition, there wouldn't be much point. Plenty of humans make it within a biologically similar structure without producing the memorization of family lines.

4. The aliens are hermaphrodites. The product of a first birth "carries the line." Such an offspring must memorize the family line; products of subsequent births become "line founders." They must memorize nothing, but must, instead, begin their own lines in an honorable fashion.

5. Back up a bit. One of the alien adults has given birth; its first live delivery after four attempts. This child, if it lives, will be the one who carries the line for the thousandth generation—a very special child. But will it live?

6. A scene in a hut of some sort—almost primitive. The parent is waiting for word to come from the village priests. Is the child worthy? Another priest waits with the parent. Who wants priests? I don't.

7. Begin with the child just before it must go off to school to learn its lessons—boarding school . . . We could call it Oxford. Try again.

8. The biological and social imperatives behind the custom would not be consistent with sending the offspring into any kind of group education. Where to go?

9. Make notes and consign to story dump.

FILE #5

Starting Point:

Saw Lee Marvin movie. WW II and he is stranded on an island with a Japanese soldier. Initial conflict, mutual abuse, then they must work together to get off the island. The ending was unconvincing, as well as being rotten. But I like the theme. Too bad it's old.

Initial Development:

1. Zilch. Make note and consign to story dump.

FILE #6

Starting Point:

What about that old language gimmick idea? Alien and human stranded on island, story winds up all in the alien language?

Initial Development:

1. Tried out four pages and am rolling world's largest cornball. Even with gimmick, still old idea.

2. Make note and consign to story dump.

FILE #7

Starting Point:

Looking at the stars, admiting the constellation Draco. Draco—Dracs— Dracula—Draggers. Drac as a root has threatening connotations; uncomfortable on the ear.

Initial Development:

1. Draco is on the outside of the galaxy. If anybody lives there and wants to expand, they are going to have to come through us.

2. Eltanin, the Dragon's nose, is a K5 star; orange, about 5,100 degrees—900 less than the Sun. A planet close enough would be just about right.

3. For what? "War In Space?" Note and consign to story dump.

FILE #8

Starting Point:

Old ghost coming back to haunt me. 1970 or thereabouts in correspondence with several persons on the subject of a "practical philosophy." Threw out letters long ago, but general sentiment expressed was an overwhelming exasperation with "nonexistent black cat," "angels on pinhead" philosophical hair-splitting. A strong desire for a philosophy—a set of rules—that can be used for conducting one's life. A "living" philosophy. Nontheistic; we're all atheists under the self-delusions. Burned up all of my own writings on the subject when I gave up being Crusader Rabbit to write SF. Turgid stuff anyway. But the need is still there.

The whole race is still groping around, killing itself, driving itself into poverty, forcing war in the name of "national interest," "honor," "fairness," and "justice." Meanwhile, the human-critters on this bouncing ball are confused, feeling helpless, watching everything going down the toilet and not knowing what to do. The ones who aren't confused are deluded. "If you aren't depressed, you just don't know what's going on." In the midst of all this, can a workable philosophy—personally, individually workable—be devised?

Initial Development:

1. C'mon storyteller. Philosophies are arguments to justify moralities: sets of rules. Just like the rules for writing a story. What is the purpose of the story? What is the purpose of the morality? What goal is it that the characters on this planet seek; for which they need a rule recipe to achieve? A moral roadmap to that pot of gold, and that pot of gold is . . . what it has always been: to be happy; to feel good about yourself; to be proud; to be free . . . of what?

2. Strange word, "free." I wonder how many despotic regimes have achieved power riding on that word. "Freedom" has such strong individual meaning, but little that any two persons can agree upon when it comes to living together within the same galaxy.

3. And so this alien shows up and says "Be moral." Recall those friends who tried "grokking" after Heinlein's *Stranger In A Strange Land* came out? The money bowl. Put in what you earn; take out what you need. After a while they discovered some were always putting in while others did all the taking out.

4. Rand's *Atlas Shrugged.* The only trouble with Rand's brand of "freedom" is having to take your brain to the cleaners weekly. Libertarians and Randroids. Always walking around muttering to themselves; worrying about everyone else's lack of morals. Never met a bigger bunch of crooks in my life. I don't mind being ripped off half as much as being forced to listen while the thief bores me

to death explaining why it was "moral" for him to lift my leather.

5. Look, stupid. Remember why you chucked this stuff to write SF? Make note and consign to story dump, if not the trash can.

FILE #9

Starting Point:

My dentist has his act together better than anyone I know. Aside from making a fortune (which I am certain is secondary to him), he really loves his work. He wears out two shifts of dental assistants every day and is going stronger at the end of the day than at the beginning. He has found his place in this universe and is filling it with a vengeance. Envying him his happiness was one of the major reasons I took the leap—quit the printing business and went full-time into writing even before my first story sold. To be doing what I wanted to do, rather than what would be "practical." Searching for a similar happiness. My place in this universe.

Initial Development:

1. Put together an alien and a human. They are in some kind of dire situation, but the alien has his act together—has a well of strength he can draw from. The human does not. The human . . . is human.

2. Willis E. Davidge. Born . . . in Kansas. Vague, gray, uninspiring parents, childhood, education, and life. Why Kansas? A lot of gray fictional childhoods happen in the midwest. Dorothy in *The Wizard of Oz* came from Kansas. Kansas is almost synonymous with the blahs. Someday the people in Kansas are going to form an action group to get the state's image changed.

3. Davidge, Willis E. Don't know where the name comes from. Rootless, doesn't make lasting friendships, insecure, defensive, quick to anger (sound familiar?).

4. The alien. Forget form. What does this critter know? Why is he secure? Where does his character, his strength come from? It must be something the human can learn, hence it cannot be a thing peculiar to that race of aliens. Philosophy. What does the alien believe? How has he been reared? Give this a rest and work on the story situation.

5. What dire situation are they in? How do we throw these two characters together? What about the language gimmick, space negotiation thing? Davidge could be the human negotiation chief while the alien . . .

6. The image I have of Willis E. Davidge rebels at being a diplomat. Not only wouldn't he like it, he wouldn't be any good at it. The space shuttle thing is too immediate a danger. Davidge would be too busy trying to save his hide and learn a language to learn what the alien has to teach—whatever that is. It's hard to reflect upon philosophy when the air is running out.

7. A less immediate danger. A situation that allows the characters to sit, talk. It could be in a larger vessel. But it can't be in a ship. The readers would keep expecting either someone to come along, our heroes to be sucked into a black hole, or a brilliant technological rabbit out of the hat to save their respective bacons. I would be expecting it, myself. If the alien has something to teach, it must be in an environment that will not cause the reader to expect anything from outside. The two characters must be stuck, permanently. They must be

stuck in a situation that allows them to talk, but the environment must be such that it does not detract from the talk.

8. Prison? A far future Chateau D'If with W. Edmund Davidge entombed with a tentacled L'Abbe Faria? Monte Crisco's Flying Circus? W. Edmund escapes, flees to L'Abbe's secret island on the planet France (homeland of the Coneheads) and takes possession of his teacher's vast fortune: a cave full of walnuts. "I'll be damned," reflected W. Edmund. "That old sucker *was* mad!"

No, I don't think so.

9. Can't get the image of the alien in my head. The alien doesn't exist yet. That includes his beliefs—the stuff Davidge will learn. Maybe I am blinding myself with the language gimmick. If an alien (or another human for all that matters) whipped an answer on me that would guide me in securing my own place in this universe, what would that answer be? Big blank. What is life? "Life is like a sewer. You only get out of it what you put into it."—Tom Lehrer.

10. Consign to story dump.

FILE #10

Starting Point:

Snow. Snow, snow, and more snow. Maine winters are brutal things. Killers. Thirty-two below zero this morning and winds that must be doing twenty miles per hour at least. I can't remember the formula, but the wind chill factor must be off the chart again. It strains the imagination that the Passamaquoddy Indians lived here all year round when all they had to do was point their moccasins south. I suppose the Seminoles would get testy about the Passamaquoddys moving into Miami Beach, but I figure a Passamaquoddy with a minus forty degree breeze on his backside has got to be a fellow with an incentive. You don't suppose that the Passamaquoddy Indians actually *liked* it here? Could be. Their descendants have an army of lawyers suing the state to get their icebox back.

Initial Development:

1. What must it be like to withstand a Maine winter under primitive conditions? With insulation, central heating backed up by wood stoves, and never leaving the house, I can barely stand it.

2. Primitive conditions. No canned food, no preservatives, no down-filled parkas, no twelve-hour cold capsules (God! My sinuses!). Growing up under those conditions and being trained to do the things one must do to survive probably takes the scare out of it. But what if I, right now, had to go out there and survive with only the knowledge I have at this moment? I wouldn't last twenty-four hours.

3. Give yourself a break. Start in summer. You know winter is coming and you must prepare for it. What could I do? What do I know how to do? First, a shelter; and remember this is Maine. I'm not going to be able to get away with a tent or lean to. No cloth for the tent anyway. Animal skins could make a tent. The easiest skins to work with (that come in large pieces) tend to come wrapped around large animals. Bear, moose, deer—I have a mental picture of myself trying to bring down a black bear by bopping it on the head with a rock. The bear turns around and says "What?"

I shrug, grin, hold my hands behind my back. "Nothing. Just looking for a little conversation. I was bored."

The bear laughs, and as he lumbers off I hear him say, "If you think Maine is boring, you should see Kansas."

4. A cave for a shelter—one with a water supply. It's either that or melt snow, and I don't have anything to melt it in. Sanitation. Going out in *that* to relieve myself? It's either that or stink up the cave. What did the Passamaquoddys do? What they did was to install indoor plumbing about ten minutes after it was invented. Put that one aside for a while.

5. Small animals for skins and food. Sew the little buggers together with strips of skin or plant fibers. Use bone needle. I'll need warm clothing. That's right! The down from mature milkweed pods can be used for insulation. Good old survival training. A double suit of skins quilted with pod down between. Scrape and dry the skins. Have to peg them out, otherwise they'll shrink to nothing. How to preserve food? Don't have to preserve onions and potatoes. Wild onions and start checking out those roots. Dried mushrooms? I don't know enough about mushrooms to distinguish the edible from the deadly. Back to preserving meat. Salt? Yecch! Smoking? What wood? I've heard of hickory smoked hams and Mainers smoke some kind of fish with alders. Fishing is easier than bopping bears with rocks. I'll need another cave for a smokehouse.

6. Fill up the cave with firewood (Oops. Have to find another cave. Need one with an outlet for the smoke). A large piece of slate for a griddle, a bed of pine branches, plenty of chow stored up. And now what?

7. I sit on it for five straight months and go stark staring bonkers from boredom. No. Not boredom. Loneliness. I have me for company, and I've never been comfortable with that situation.

8. This is a perfect situation for the alien with the answers to begin jawing with the human who has the need.

[Here I went back and took another look at File #9.]

9. This is the situation—the setting. Hostile enough to drive the two together, but dull, dull, dull. The characters and what the characters say and do will stand out against this kind of bleak, deadly motonony.

10. So I'm camping in a cave (Why? Where? Who knows?) and along comes this alien, see. (From where? Why?) And the alien says "What are you? Some kind of nut living like that?"

And I scream, "Talk to me! Tell me the answer! Talk to me! I'm *bored!*"

The alien walks off saying, "You think you're bored? I just spent a week in Kansas." The alien meets the bear, they have so much in common they get married and have a litter of hairy toadstools.

11. How do we get those two characters together in that situation? Another planet? Strand them on another planet? I smell two enemies being stranded together in a hostile environment; they must put aside their feelings and co-operate if they are to survive.

[Here I went back and checked File #5.]

12. I still like the theme, but it's still old. Besides, I still don't see the alien. I especially don't know what answers he has for the human. How can he have the answers? The human doesn't even know what questions to ask!

14. Why did I start this? Oh yeah. The snow. It's still snowing. It will keep this up for months. Consign to story dump.

FILE #11

Starting Point:

Thinking about that image of the human bending over the dying alien again, the alien eliciting a promise of some kind from the human. Tonight David Niven playing in *The Best of Enemies* on the tube. A title popped into my head: "Enemy Mine." Nice-sounding title.

Initial Development:

1. Consign to story dump.

THE STEWING OF "ENEMY MINE"

File #11 was the last written note I made before beginning my novella "Enemy Mine" about a month later. I referred to none of the notes above in writing the story. In fact, I had forgotten about all of them (they were mixed in with about twenty-five hundred similar notes). I didn't realize that I had borrowed from all of the notes above until I began doing the research for this chapter. In comparing the notes with the finished story, however, I found that some of the things that were borrowed were considerably altered. This suggested to me that between the last note and the first page of the manuscript an unconscious metamorphosis had taken place—a "stewing period." Below I have listed the parts from the notes that were used, and in brackets are mentions regarding the use of those parts in the story.

FILE #1: The alien language. [Since I did not refer to either the structure or vocabulary I had invented, both changed considerably. The version appearing in the story is more easily pronounced. A few obscenities in the language were added.] The brotherhood of creatures, we're all in this together theme. [No changes. An old theme, but aren't they all? It isn't blatant in the story, but rides just under the surface.]

FILE #2: The different perceptions two individuals can have of the same object, issue, or event. [Because of the physiological, cultural, and philosophical differences between the two characters, this theme was considerably developed.]

FILE #3: Image of a human bending over an alien. The alien is dying. The alien elicits a promise from the human. [No real change, but considerably developed because in the story we know the two characters and the meaning of the promise.]

FILE #4: The hermaphroditic alien culture where, to achieve adulthood, the one who "carries the line" must recite it. In this culture the line *is* identity. [Main changes are the development of the alien's parent, culture, and home, and the switch from an almost primitive culture to a modern one highly respectful of anything ancient (traditions, family lines, buildings, teachings).]

FILE #5: Two enemies stranded on an island in a hostile environment. They must work together to achieve their goals. [Theme swiped intact for main story line.]

FILE #6: Same thing as #5 with the addition of the language exercise (winding up the story in the alien language). [I discarded trying to teach the language, but used the initial attempts at conversation to open the story and follow through with a mutual pidgin language. From the beginning of the second quarter, since they each knew the other's language, I mostly used English when either language was being spoken unless it was imperative that the reader know that the dialog was in the alien language.]

FILE #7: The constellation Draco. Eltanin, home star of the Dracs (aliens). Eltanin's second planet is their home. The race has a tradition of exploration (as do humans) and both races run into each other in their expansion efforts. [Swiped intact. It is not a space war story, but the war is the "frame situation" that gets the characters into their particular conflict.]

FILE #8: The need for a usable "practical" philosophy. [*The Talman*, a non-theistic "bible" containing the works of several great Drac philosophers. Its message is life in the here-and-now rooted in a combination of the logic of contexts, general semantics, and some extensive work I had done in the past on problem solving strategies. The philosophy rests on two apparently contradictory thrusts: an almost fanatic individualism combined with an equally fanatic devotion to the family line. The issue of identity shows these to be mutually serving rather than contradictory. To enter adulthood, not only must the family line be memorized, *The Talman* must be memorized as well. I am not certain, but I feel that I could sit down and write the entire book within two months, I know it so well. It is not my philosophy—I'm not well enough organized to have one worth sharing—it was invented for the story. However, I might adopt it myself some-day.]

FILE #9: A man who has found his place in this universe and is secure in it [the character of the alien] being envied by one who is still groping around [the character of the human]. Willis E. Davidge, rootless, friendless, insecure, defensive, quick to anger, hails from Kansas. [Davidge is the human's name. His history was considerably developed.] Where does the alien's strength of character come from? What does he believe? [See *The Talman* in File #8 above.] They (the characters) must be in a situation that allows them to talk, but that will not detract from the talk. [See File #10 Below.]

FILE #10. The dreary but deadly Maine winter and the speculations on how to survive it under primitive conditions. [The environment and survival techniques were swiped intact. The setting is on Fyrine IV, a long winter, short summer planet with a rotation half that of Earth's; about ninety percent covered with water, constant high winds, stormy seas, and cloudy skies—making the setting even drearier, and deadlier. Lifeforms peculiar to the planet were invented, but nothing weird, wonderful, or frightening. That would have defeated the story's purpose].

FILE #11. The title: "Enemy Mine." [Swiped intact.]

THE WRITING OF "ENEMY MINE"

Remember that when I sat down to write this story, everything under "stewing" above was held in my subconscious. When my fingers touched the keys, I had a character—Willis E. Davidge, downed fighter pilot, pulling himself onto a beach to have it out with his enemy. I had no idea what that enemy was going to be or look like. Then Davidge opened his eyes, I saw the creature at the same time, and the writing began:

The Dracon's three-fingered hands flexed. In the thing's yellow eyes I could read the desire to have those fingers either around a weapon or my throat. As I flexed my own fingers, I knew it read the same in my eyes.

"Irkmaan!" the thing spat.

"You piece of Drac slime." I brought my hands up in front of my chest and waved the thing on. "Come on, Drac; come and get it."

"Irkmaan vaa, koruum su!"

"Are you going to talk or fight? Come on!" . . .

[At this point I briefly backfilled to establish that they were opposing fighter pilots, had caused each other to go down, and were stranded on a tiny wind and water-swept island. I still didn't know where the story was going.]

. . . The Drac just stood there and I went over the phrase taught us in training—a phrase calculated to drive any Drac into a frenzy. *"Kiz da Yuomeen, Shizumaat!"* Meaning: Shizumaat, the most revered Drac philosopher, eats Kiz excrement. Something on the level of stuffing a Moslem full of pork.

The Drac opened its mouth in horror, then closed it as black anger literally changed its color from yellow to reddish-brown. *"Irkmaan, yaa* stupid Mickey Mouse is!"

[After that, I had no control over the characters whatsoever. I learned the alien's name when Davidge learned it. Jeriba Shigan. After some initial skull-thumping, then almost getting killed by a tidal wave, the pair move Jeriba Shigan's ejection capsule to the highest point on the island and build a stone shack around it. It takes time, they are still enemies, but their language is evolving.]

I threw down the splinter. "Damn, I hate this place!"

"Ess?" Jerry's head poked around the edge of the [shack's] opening. "Who talking at, Davidge?"

I glared at the Drac, then waved my hand at it. "Nobody."

"Ess va 'nobody'?"

"Nobody. Nothing."

"Ne gavey, Davidge."

I poked my chest with my finger. "Me! I'm talking to myself! You *gavey* that stuff, toadface!"

Jerry shook its head. "Davidge, now I sleep. Talk not so much nobody, *ne?"*

[Later the two seek refuge in the capsule during a particularly bad storm. Davidge learns that the alien is pregnant. They are washed off the island, and Davidge is injured and becomes unconscious. He awakens from a coma almost an Earth month later. Davidge learns that they are on a larger land mass, and that the Drac has nursed him back to health. Once Davidge is on his feet again, the pair realize that the planet has a winter and they begin preparing for it. They find a cave and set up housekeeping, having stocked the cave with firewood, roots, and preserved snakemeat. Then they sit, killing time by making things out of snakeskin, and by talking. By now they are familiar with each other's language.]

We talked of Jerry's coming child:

"What are you going to name it, Jerry?"

"It already has a name. See, the Jeriba line has five names. My name is Shigan; before me came my parent, Gothig; before Gothig was Haesni; before Haesni was Ty, and before Ty was Zammis. The child is named Jeriba Zammis."

"Why only the five names? A human child can have just about any name its parents pick for it. In fact, once a human becomes an adult, he or she can pick any name he or she wants."

The Drac looked at me, its eyes filled with pity. "Davidge, how lost you must feel. You humans—how lost you must feel."

"Lost?"

Jerry nodded. "Where do you come from, Davidge?"

"You mean my parents?"

"Yes."

I shrugged. "I remember my parents."

"And their parents?"

"I remember my mother's father. When I was young we used to visit him."

"Davidge, what do you know about this grandparent?"

I rubbed my chin. "It's kind of vague . . . I think he was in some kind of agriculture."

"And his parents?"

I shook my head. "The only thing I remember is that somewhere along the line, English and Germans figured. *Gavey* Germans and English?"

Jerry nodded. "Davidge, I can recite the history of my line back to the founding of my planet by Jeriba Ty, one of the original settlers, one hundred and ninety-nine generations ago. . . . [Jeriba Shigan continues explaining Drac lines and their significance.]

I went over to my bed and stretched out. As I stared up at the smoke being sucked through the crack in the chamber's ceiling, I began to understand what Jerry meant by feeling lost. A Drac with several dozens of generations under his belt knew who it was and what it had to live up to. . . . [Davidge asks the Drac to recite its line, and Jeriba Shigan recites] . . . As I listened to Jerry's singsong of formal Dracon, the backward biographies—beginning with death and ending with adulthood—I experienced a sense of timebinding, of being able to know and touch the past. Battles, empires built and destroyed, discoveries made, great things done—a tour through twelve thousand years of history, but perceived as a well-defined, living continuum.

Against this: I Willis of the Davidge line stand before you, born of

Sybil the housewife and Nathan the second-rate civil e
them born of Grandpop, who probably had something
riculture, born of nobody in particular . . . Hell, I was
My older brother carried the line; not me. I listened an
mind to memorize the line of Jeriba.

[The winter drags on, the alien grows heavier as its pregnancy comes to term,
and the two talk of many things. In a moment of depression, the Drac pulls out
a small golden cube that it wears suspended from a chain around its neck. It
contains the Drac's *Talman*, the writings of the great Drac philosophers. The
Drac explains what the thing is and offers to teach Davidge to read it. When
Davidge agrees, the Drac loans him its *Talman*. Davidge sets out to memorize
that as well. The winter seems endless, and the Drac gets heavier and very sick.
The firewood runs out, and Davidge must go outside every so often to beat the
ice off the dead standing trees and gather more wood. He is at this task when
he hears a scream coming from the cave. He drops everything and runs into
the cave. The Drac is writhing in pain.]

I dropped on my knees next to the Drac. "I'm here, Jerry. What is
it? What's wrong?"
"Davidge!" The Drac rolled its eyes, seeing nothing, its mouth
worked silently, then exploded with another scream.
"Jerry, it's me!" I shook the Drac's shoulder. "It's me, Jerry. Dav-
idge!"
Jerry turned its head toward me, grimaced, then clasped the fingers
of one hand around my left wrist with the strength of pain. "Davidge!
Zammis . . . something's gone wrong!"
"What? What can I do?"
Jerry screamed again, then its head fell back to the bed in a half-
faint. The Drac fought back to consciousness and pulled my head down
to its lips. "Davidge, you must swear."
"What, Jerry? Swear what?"
"Zammis . . . on Draco. To stand before the line's archives. Do this."
"What do you mean? You talk like you're dying."
"I am, Davidge. Zammis two hundredth generation . . . very impor-
tant. Present my child, Davidge. Swear!"

Jeriba Shigan dies and Davidge successfully delivers the Drac child, Zammis.
At this point in the writing the manuscript was over twelve thousand words
long, and I had been at my typewriter thirty-two hours straight. I remembered
the image I once had about a human bending over a dying alien; the alien
eliciting a promise from the human. That, in adiditon to being tired and having
gotten to know Jeriba Shigan very well, started me crying. But when I realized
the stark loneliness now facing the character of Davidge, I immediately went
into a deep depression. That's when I went to bed. After I awakened, I could
take a colder look at the story. It would have to wind up soon. It was intended
for a magazine and it was already over twelve thousand words long. Instead of
continuing to let the characters run the story, I assumed control, cooked up an

asy ending, then sent the manuscript off. The draft ran to a little over sixteen thousand words.

I didn't want to ache with Davidge in his loneliness. Immediately he transfers his need for companionship into love for the alien child. He teaches the child the line and *The Talman*, time passes, the kid finds a mess of valuable gemstones, a survey team finds them, takes Zammis off to Draco, while Davidge stays on Fyrine IV. More time passes, a ship lands and it's Jeriba Gothig (Shigan's parent) and Zammis. Davidge stands with Zammis for the recital before the family archives, now located on Fyrine IV. End of story.

THE REWRITING OF "ENEMY MINE" #1

The manuscript had a lot going for it, but something didn't sit well with George Scithers. He sent it to Isaac Asimov for a reading. Isaac Asimov wrote back, saying some nice things, but in addition that it looked like what I had was two different stories. He suggested ending the first story with the death of the alien, then doing a sequel centered on the alien child. Back it came.

I hacked the story off with the death of the alien, sent it off, and it was accepted under the title "Enemy Mine." Then ensued four of the most miserable months of my life. I could not get started on the sequel. It was under the working title "A Promise To Keep." I couldn't get into it for two reasons: First, ending the first story with the death of the Drac and Davidge still stuck on the planet bothered me. It's just not my kind of ending. Second, the characters had become distant.

I did not want to climb back into Davidge's skin. Stuck alone in a hostile but dreary environment with an infant on my hands and my only friend dead just about fills every requirement I have for my grandaddy of all nightmares. I burned up close to twenty thousand words worth of false starts on the sequel. I tried changing the point of view several times, took my original ending and tried to fatten it up with more words, and nothing worked. Nothing worked until I decided to take my lumps, climb back into Davidge's skin, and continue the story. I took the last page of "Enemy Mine," ran it through the typewriter again, and continued.

It stumbled around some because, as a separate story, I had to re-establish the story situation and backfill everything that had gone on before. But on it went. I know old Davidge. His first impulse after the death of his friend wouldn't be to love the child; he'd *hate* it—blame it for the death of Jeriba Shigan. I stood in the background and let the characters take over again. Almost three days straight at the typewriter, and I had finished (no, I'm not going to reveal the ending. Buy *Manifest Destiny* [Berkley Books] and read it for yourself!).

THE REWRITING OF "ENEMY MINE" #2

When I sent off the sequel, something still bothered me: ending the first story with the death of Jeriba Shigan. I called George, informed him that the manuscript was on its way and suggested that he consider running the two stories together as a single piece. Not likely. It would make a story 30,000 words long, taking up half of an entire issue.

Time passed. George Scithers called and told me that he was running it as a single story. What decided him was letting one of his assistant editors, Lee Weinstein, read the opening, then asking him "What's happening in the story?"

The answer was "Well, this guy's just killed this alien and is feeling pretty bad about it."

To put the two stories together, I cut out all of the backfilling I had done in the second part. It appeared under the title "Enemy Mine" in the September 1979 issue of *IA'sfm*.

THE METHOD ADAPTED

I did not plan the method I use for writing; it evolved. It wasn't until I wrote this chapter that I realized how entrenched this method is, nor how well it works—for me. It may or may not work for you. To try it, keep an idea file; what I call my "story dump." Keep putting in your ideas, bits of dialog, character sketches, rejected stories, newspaper clippings—whatever strikes you. Don't be concerned about the slightness of the things you put into your file. No one ever has to see it except you; and those trivial things can grow to become giants if left alone to mature.

The method described above doesn't have to be as haphazard as it appears. You needn't sit around feeding your story dump waiting for "inspiration" to strike. If you have a starting premise that you wish to construct a story with, create a file for that premise; then begin feeding that file with everything related to that premise that you can dream up. For example, the premise of "Homecoming" was suggested by George Scithers: intelligent dinosaurs that show up in the present to reclaim their planet. I had nothing else to work with.

I began collecting everything I could find on dinosaurs, and the period during which the dinosaurs lived, and spent a lot of time thinking about the here and now. Once they showed up and discovered that another intelligent race had evolved on Earth, what would the dinosaurs do? What would the humans do in response? Ideas, bits and snatches of dialog, a dozen character sketches went into the file. One character sketch ran to over a thousand words; when the character appeared in the story he said one line, then exited.

I call this "iceberging." Only a little piece of the research and work actually appears in the story; the rest is beneath the surface. Iceberging your characters, settings, situations, and premises has two results: the little bit that appears in the story "feels" substantive—convincing—to the reader; in addition, if you have to move the scene, change characters, develop an interesting situation, you will be dealing at all times with familiar territory, people, and information. You know how a character will react within a given situation because you *know* the character *and* the situation.

Feeding the information file, although more narrowly confined, is essentially the same process that was used to set myself up to write "Enemy Mine." During the information gathering, there was a "stewing period," followed at a particular point by a strong urge to tell the story—still not knowing what the story was. The characters were placed on the paper, then off they went.

CHAPTER NINE

GETTING IT TO THE EDITOR

THE SLUSHPILE

Marine recruits begin in boot camp; business executive trainees begin on the bottom rung; unsolicited beginning manuscripts start in the editor's slushpile. All three institutions are both initiation and screening mechanisms. Graduating from any one of them means that you have met certain minimum requirements. All three look for certain uniform standards to be met before allowing graduation to occur.

A Marine boot would sooner slit his throat than show up for inspection wearing an aloha shirt; a business executive trainee would think himself insane to willingly refuse to learn and observe common business customs and practices. Many beginning writers, however, make an effort at "standing out" from the crowd; not through spellbinding storytelling, but through attempts at imaginative packaging. This leads to the use of such things as green manuscript paper, purple ribbons, and anything else that they think will make their manuscripts "unique."

The mails are choked with "unique," "individualized," manuscripts—the majority of them heading straight back to their authors. There is nothing that finds itself less unique on an editor's desk than a "unique" manuscript. You could type your story in red ink on slices of baloney and mail it in a syrup barrel and your manuscript wouldn't stand out from the sameness of the slushpile.

Anyone who has ever spent an hour or two going through an editor's slushpile (which I have done on occasion) begins to understand what readers and editors mean when they say that they can sense an amateur effort even before the envelope is opened. If one hasn't had this experience, one might think that such an attitude is very unfair. However, it is spooky—this seventh sense one develops reading manuscripts—how accurate it can be.

Let's look through the eyes of an editor and pick a submission at random from the slushpile. Now, let's see . . . The 9x12 mailer is hand-addressed (if the long axis of a 9x12 can't fit in your typewriter, use mailing labels); there are large arrows drawn on the envelope pointing at the address (yes, there are postal employees who cannot find their own faces in a mirror, but arrows will not help them to find an address); there are cute little dragons drawn on it (a threat?) or, perhaps, "happy face" stickers (a curse?); perhaps there is a message written on the outside of the envelope (that's what's supposed to be *inside* the envelope); the 9x12 is worn, beat-up, or reused from another mailing, giving the impression that the contents have already been rejected by fifty other editors (inflation notwithstanding, new 9x12's are not expensive). The envelope bellows two things almost out loud: "Hey, look at me!" and "I don't know what I'm doing!"

The editor or reader has opened thousands of similar envelopes, and 999 times out of 1,000, the contents haven't been worth reading past the first page. Perhaps that one out of a thousand might be repairable because of a good idea. Maybe one in ten thousand is worth buying as is. No matter how you look at it, this is low-grade ore. I have heard editors and readers issue unintentional sighs of extreme pain as they picked up an envelope and got their first look at it. Statistically, they know what almost *has* to be in it: drek—rank, amateur drek. But, they open it up, because there's always that slim chance.

Then out comes the manuscript: no margins, and typed off the end of the sheet with a ribbon so light there is doubt concerning the use of a ribbon at all. More sighs of pain. As bad as the odds were before the envelope was opened, the odds afterward begin dropping like the dollar. Now . . . maybe one in a million. Reading begins—

Let us end this tale of horror (how would *you* like to put in your daily eight working at a job like *that?*) and consider the simple fact that, even if this particular story is better than average, it already has a multitude of strikes against it. The red-rimmed eyes scanning those poorly typed sheets *expect* to find drek. There are a hundred more manuscripts to wade through (some with clean, typed envelopes), and all those tired eyes are looking for is an excuse to hang a rejection on the current wad of papers to get on with the next offering. Even experienced, professional writers make mistakes; and it would take one glorious piece of literary perfection to make it past an attitude such as the one described in our hypothetical peruser of slush.

Stanley Schmidt claims to have gotten the all-time horror of submission formats: "The story was a single page, typed by placing two white sheets in the typewriter with a (faded) carbon behind them—yes, behind, not between, and with the printing side on the front instead of the back—so that the whole thing appeared backward in faint and fuzzy characters." The author's note suggested that the editor use a mirror to read the manuscript. Stanley showed a lot of class in suggesting to the author only that he type his submission correctly. George H. Scithers claims the same dubious honor. The MS submitted to him was typed so that each page had to be read from page bottom to page top.

I am not a judge of contests in this vein; however, the results should be noted: yes, both editors noticed; yes, both manuscripts went streaking back to their authors with rejection slips; yes, both editors will *still* remember the *next* time these authors' literary children appear in the slushpile. I am not saying that their future stories will be rejected solely on the basis of biled memory; but their postage would be more wisely invested in pork belly futures.

There are two ways to get the editor's attention, neither of which is being an inept storyteller or an eccentric in one's choices of papers, ribbon colors, envelope decorations, or typing formats. The first part of this volume is concerned with the first way: write a professional-grade story. This chapter is concerned with the second way: conduct yourself as a professional and submit your story in a professional manner.

When you submit a manuscript, you will want the happy face on the reader; not on the envelope. You will want your words to be read with an open—even eager—mind; not with a mind contemplating matches, paper in hand, and the energy crisis. The only way to obtain the desired treatment is to submit a professional manuscript in a professional manner. To do this, it is your obligation to yourself and to your work to learn the production mechanics of your profession.

WHERE AND WHEN TO WRITE

Even before you can make it to the slushpile, the words have to make it on the paper. Where will you set up your production line, and when will you run it? I suppose every new writer has a fantasy about a natural wood interiored cabin tucked away in the woods far from anything that might interrupt the creative flow. I know several old writers who still have the same fantasy (they mutter to themselves a lot). This was a fantasy of mine. But are we not story-tellers? If we can't tell the difference between fantasy and the necessities of reality, we get sent to the lollipop factory.

My office began in the back of an H & R Block tax office: constant screams of joy at finding out how little one owes the government; more frequent howls of pain and gnashing of teeth finding out how *much* one *does* owe the government; a never-ending river of runny-nosed brats wandering around, waiting for Mommy and Daddy to finish cursing—"Hey, mistah, whatcha doin'?" —old friends wandering in, dropping into a chair— "Not disturbin' you, am I, Barry? Waitin' for my turn. Damn, but Sam is stickin' it to the farmers this year. Thinkin' o' buyin' a printin' press 'n' payin' the damn taxes that way . . ." — *"Four thousand dollars!* Wha . . . Wha . . . Waaaaaah!" — "Now, Elmer, don't play with the nice man's typewriter . . . Oh! That's one of them word processors? A *computer?* Move over, Elmer, and let me get a look at that thing . . ." — A local fan drops by, "Can't see how you can work under conditions like this . . . No, just waitin' for my turn at the tax lady . . ." — A new fan moseys in, "Are you . . . I mean . . . are you *the* Barry Longyear? I so much loved your story 'Solo.' . . . Who? . . . Steve Perry wrote that? . . . No, I'm just waiting my turn to get my taxes done . . ." — "Hey, mistah, what's all these papers what fell down?"

And I write. My office began there, and there it still remains. At this point, if I ever did get my little cabin in the woods, I'd probably go gaga from the quiet. The point of all of this is that you write where and when you can. "I have to have absolute, uninterrupted silence; an atmosphere conducive to the creative flow; a setting wherein the muse will appear" —is the cry of the I'll-Never-Be-A-Writer Bird. Where to write? Any flat surface strong enough to support a typewriter and tall enough to place underneath it a chair and a pair of knees. I have seen some writers do without the surface and make do with the knees.

When to write? You have a house to keep, children to keep out of mischief, a job to hold down, bosses, spouses, kids, and creditors nagging at you; your cat just died and the storm toppled that old oak through the roof of the house; the laundry is four feet high, the dust kitties are beginning to grow teeth and are wandering the house in search of prey; the basement floods, the school district supervisor calls and says your son has just been sacked for selling porno pictures to the first-graders and your doctor tells you that you have cancer; your parents, for the umpteenth time that week, want to know when you are going to stop fooling around and try making something of yourself; you've been disinherited, your spouse, mistress, or sugar-daddy has just walked out, your car just put out its last gasp, the Soviet Union invades Afghanistan, the world is on the brink of nuclear war—

That's when you write. If you want to write, writing has to come first, and frequently. If you wait for that tranquil moment when all the work is done, everything is in its place and all's right with your world, you will never write. That moment is a fantasy—a world you write about; not live in. Believing in that fantasy implies something else: it implies that everything else comes before writing.

There is a phrase that is inflicted upon writers every now and then by those who cherish this little lie that they too could become writers "If I only had your time." A science teacher once said this to me, and I replied: "If I only had *your* time, I'd be a science teacher." You pick your course and you spend your time accordingly. Whether you write full-time or part-time, *"time"* is the key word.

Writing time is not something that will present itself and say "It's time to write." Writing time is something that has to be carved out of each day with a meat axe, and woe be to those who get in the way of that blade. Yes, it will be hard on those around you, and even harder on yourself. But writing is an *art*, and you are working to become an *artist*, not a social welfare flunky. Yes, it is selfish. The production of art is the most selfish thing in the world. Your art, after it has been produced, may bring joy and warmth to thousands—even millions; but to do what needs to be done to produce that art, you must be selfish. It has a price.

TYPEWRITERS

Those who have worked the slushpile know: there are many typewritten manuscripts that come in that are harder to read than handwritten manuscripts. Also remember that handwritten manuscripts will not be read. Any make or model of typewriter, of whatever vintage, cleaned and in reasonable repair, can turn out a professional looking manuscript if the operator of that machine knows what to do. If you know how to type, consider yourself rich. If you can stall the storytelling urge long enough to take a course in touch typing, do so. Many writers (myself included) are self-taught typists. Hunting and pecking, painting out mistakes with Liquid Paper along the way, our production (daily word rate) is probably half of what it could be. If you already have a typewriter (and are not independently wealthy) you are stuck with the machine you have. Weep not. My first machine cost $20 and I sold a mess of short stories, novellas, and five novels with it.

What is reasonable repair? Does the type on your machine align properly? Are the caps a half-space above the lower case letters? Do all the keys work? Is the platen (roller) so hard and beat-up that the letter impressions are poor? Is the platen misaligned, allowing the tops of letters to be cut off? Does the space bar work only when you thump it with your thumb, or does it throw in spaces at random? Does the ribbon advance only work when you spin the take-up wheel with your finger? As a writer, you will have enough troubles without the additional bother of a poorly working machine. Get it fixed. Reasonable repair means the same thing that it does in the service about rifles and other weapons. For those who haven't had service experience, it means this: if you want to stay alive, your machine had best work properly.

If you do not have a typewriter, shop around before buying. The demands writers put on typewriters are different than those put on by secretaries or college students rapping out term papers. Try out everything before you lay down your money. New typewriters today run from around $80 for junk to over a thousand dollars for an electric with self-correcting ribbon, memory, and a pretty paint job. You are the one who will have to operate the machine, so find a machine that will produce handsomely done type, is comfortable to operate, and is within your budget. My advice: do not buy on time; there are enough pressures involved in breaking into writing without having a machine looking at you crying "Pay for me!" Other writers consider a wolf waiting at the door an incentive—an oar in the creative flow.

TYPING HINTS

When purchasing a machine, or considering a typeface for a machine that has the capacity to exchange type faces (such as IBM's Selectric), *never* pick an italic typeface, nor one of the "handwriting" faces. There is always the chance that an editor will want to purchase the story you have submitted—but *not* if you get cute with typefaces. Inserting an italic face where you want italics to appear in the story may look like extra effort in good faith to you, but to a typesetter it looks like gibberish. Hence, to the editor it looks amateur. Good old regular typewriter type, either pica or elite, is the *rule*. Italics are indicated by underscoring; *that* the typesetter understands. Also, to save trouble for everyone, make certain that the upper case "I" is distinguishable from the lower case "1."

What is a clean typewriter? There is a kind of cleaning, done by repair persons, that keeps the keys working. There is another kind of cleaning, done by you, that keeps the type readable. Any machine using a cloth ribbon will eventually transfer ink to the type faces, packing dried ink into the letters, making "o" look like a huge period and "e" indistinguishable from a packed-in "o." Like this: "●." This is hard on the eyes. Type cleaners of many sorts are available; and for very old, dried-in ink, all you have to do is take a needle and pop out the old ink. Then regular cleanings will keep the type sharp and clear—provided that you change the ribbon regularly.

Making a good impression is what it's all about. Change ribbons frequently. A ribbon that has 25 or 30 thousand words on it will suit a secretary for another 25 or 30 thousand words; as a writer, best you should change the ribbon. If your story is purchased, numbers of electrostatic copies will have to be made from your manuscript. The artist gets one, perhaps the publisher gets one, maybe the editor makes one just in case the typesetting house loses the original. Black type reproduces well; graying type does not.

The correcting of typing errors is almost a writing sub-craft. First, do not use "easy erase" paper. The stuff is hard to handle, it has a special coating that smears the ink and makes fingers sticky, it has poor opacity (it ain't white enough) making it harder to read, and editors hate it. Editors also hate erasing of any kind because the ragged, smeared results make for poor reproduction with a copying machine. It is perfectly all right to **X** out errors, providing you have only two or three such instances per page. You may also use correcting tape. It comes in rolls and you correct an error by slipping a piece of the tape between the ribbon and paper, then typing over the mistake.

Do not use Liquid Paper unless you know how. The most frequent mistake made by Liquid Paper users is not reading the instructions. You have to dab—not brush—the stuff on. If you brush it on, it will mix with the ink instead of covering it, producing a gray smear. It dries fast either in the bottle or on the paper; therefore close the bottle tightly after each use. Buy the little bottle of thinner. After several openings and closings of the bottle, Liquid Paper begins to thicken. If you do not thin the stuff, the error you paint out will look like a small snow-and-rock-covered hill, making the typed-in correction unreadable.

Mostly to make word count estimates easier, but also to maintain a sufficient margin of white space at the bottom of each page, you will want each page to have the same number of lines. Two methods: (1) Take a ream of typing paper, measure off an inch from the bottom, then run a laundry marker down the edges of the sheets. When you see the mark, put your last line next to it, then put in a new sheet. (2) Back up the sheet you are typing on with a typing guide. The kind I made up was a piece of paper, 9"x11" and ruled on *both* sides as

Fig. 9/1, Typing Guide

(Rule <u>both</u> sides identically)

shown in the illustration. No matter how you face the guide, this will give you a half-inch wide line indicator sticking out at the right showing placements for first line, chapter headings, page center, and end of page.

FIVE CAUTIONS

New developments in any form of art should cause interest in the artist, and the newest development in the production of writing is the word processor. Word processing setups can be scrounged together for as little as $2,000 on up to the stratosphere. If you are interested in a word processor, every manufacturer has paid people on staff who can explain the things better than I can. Caution #1: watch out for the printer you buy. Manuscripts printed with dot-matrix printers, because they produce almost unreadable images, are totally unacceptable at *Analog*. George Scithers at *IA'sfm* says he won't reject a manuscript *just* because it's done on a dot-matrix printer, *BUT* he doesn't *like* them. You should see the way George utters this liberal, understanding policy; he speaks in italics. Get the message?

Caution #2: make certain that your program and printer can handle upper *and* lower case type. Manuscripts done in all upper case are acceptable nowhere. Caution #3: make certain that the printed-out upper case "I" is different from the lower case "l." Caution #4: with a word processor, you will have the capability to do justified type (both left and right margins even). *Don't* use it; it fouls up word counts. Caution #5: automatic hyphenation capability; *don't* use it; hyphenating a word so it begins at the end of a line and concludes at the start of the next line is more trouble than it's worth. The word you hyphenated to get more on a line might be typeset thusly: Hyphen-ated. Remember to separate pages.

MANUSCRIPT FORMATS & PREPARATION

Page Formats: Maintain at least a one inch margin on all sides, type (one side of the sheet only) double spaced between lines (not between words) with black ink on good quality white paper of at least 16 pound weight. Indent five spaces at each new paragraph. Do not use "easy erase" paper. Avoid end-of-line hyphenation. Head every page, except the title page, in the upper right-hand corner with your last name, a word from your story title, and the sheet's page number as shown in Figure 9/2. This makes life easier for both editor and typesetter, since the manuscript will be paper-clipped in the upper left-hand corner for the editor, and stapled there for the typesetter. Remember not to place the header too close to the edge of the page. Otherwise an inaccurate copying machine may cut it off.

If you use a separate title page, begin page #1 with your first page of text. This is to simplify word count estimates. End your story by dropping three lines beneath your last line of text, centering the word "END" beneath it, and indicating that the word is not to be typeset as is shown in Figure 9/3. The upside down pigtail indicates to the typesetter that everything encircled is to be deleted.

Figures 9/4A through 9/4C are suggested page formats for separate title page, title page combined with text, and subsequent pages. When using a separate title page, note that the first page of text uses the subsequent page format (full page). This also simplifies word count estimates. Use the following method for

Fig. 9/2, Manuscript Page Header

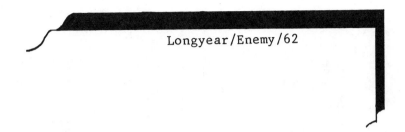

Longyear/Enemy/62

Fig. 9/3, END

and as the sun sank slowly in the west, John and Mary lived happily forever after.

END

obtaining your word count: (1) take an average page of copy, and rule a vertical line through the ragged right ends of the lines at about the average line length; (2) count the number of characters and spaces in your average line; (3) multiply this number by the number of lines per page; (4) divide by six (this gives you the number of words per page); (5) multiply your words-per-page figure by the number of pages, taking half-pages into account. This will give you your total word count. Round off to the nearest hundred and include it on your title page as shown.

MAILERS

Do not bind your submissions. Shorter works need only a paper clip; longer works like complete novels should be mailed loose in a box of the proper size (such as those that typing paper comes in). Manuscripts of five pages or less can be folded in thirds and mailed in a #10 (letter-sized) envelope. The self-addressed return envelope, with stamps *attached,* should be folded in thirds and stuck inside. Longer works should be mailed flat (either in a 9"x12" envelope or a box).

Manuscripts mailed in 9x12's should have a 9x12 return envelope, stamps *attached,* folded in half and stuck inside. Note that the Post Office charges extra for some weights of oversized envelopes. Use new envelopes, type the address parallel with the envelope's long axis, and make certain the address is the proper one (offices move), that it is being directed to the proper editor (a publishing house is a mansion of many departments), and that it is being directed to the *current* editor (they move around a lot). Be very wary about having weird stationery printed up.

Always keep a copy of the manuscript for yourself, and *always* enclose a self-addressed stamped envelope of the proper size for the return of your manu-

Barry B. Longyear
One Wilton Road
Farmington, Maine 04938

Agent:
Adele Leone Agency, Inc.,
52 Riverside Drive #6A
New York NY 10024

Approximately
12,000 Words

/ Single space all information above title;/
/ round off word count to nearest hundred; /
/ note all margins. /

THE CON TOWER CAPER

By

Barry B. Longyear

This is an example of the format to be used for a separate title page. Single space your real name and address in the upper left-hand corner (I include my agent's as well to remind folks where to sent the checks and paperwork). Almost half-way down and centered, put the story's title in all caps; double space, center the word "By," double space again and center your real name or pen name as shown. Do not number the title page. If you use a separate title page, the first page of text is page #1.

When appropriate, use this area for copyright notice, rights offered, etc.

Barry B. Longyear
One Wilton Road
Farmington, Maine 04938

Agent:
Adele Leone Agency, Inc.
52 Riverside Drive, #6A
New York NY 10024

Approximately
12,000 Words

/ If you use a combined title/beginning of text /
/ format, the title page is page #1. Note all /
/ margins. Remaining pages use the subsequent /
/ page format.

THE CON TOWER CAPER

By

Barry B. Longyear

The Con Tower was on a phoney concrete and plastic mountaintop at the end of Gernsbeck Road north of the city. The tower itself looked like a cross between a spaceship, a junkyard, and a nightmare designed by a twelve-year-old kid after chewing one of those funny mushrooms. I'd put up my bags in some Con Hotels before -- if you want to work a swank place, you have to do a Con -- but this one was straight out of a funnybook. I'd gotten a fat retainer mailed to my office. It was a cashier's check for five thousand credits and from the Con mob itself. The note that came along with that scrap full of pretty numbers said for me to pull into the Con Tower's underground garage, point my toes at the elevator marked "private," then take it to the only floor at which it would stop: the top.

I had a bunch of question marks rattling around in my skull, but I went. The main reason I steered my electric into that garage was a quick

Longyear/Tower/3

doors opened and I was facing a two and a half meter tall pile of muscles wearing long black hair, a mean-looking pig sticker, and not much else.

"Please come this way, Mr. Harlow. I'm Bruce; Ms. Suzzi's secretary."

I leaned against the doorjamb, counted my eyebrows, then staggered out of the elevator. The doors hissed shut behind me. I held my arms out and my eyes shut until my Alpo settled. That over, I looked up at Bruce's smiling face from underneath the brim of my hat. "Tell me, Bruce, (urp), Do you dress like that all the time?"

He pulled his pig sticker -- it had a blade on it longer than my arm -- and began swinging it around his head, an insane wildness contorting his barbaric features. Instinctively I reached beneath my blue-grey, polyester, double-breasted for my blaster and trained the weapon's double-bladed Norrison peep sights between Bruce's flashing brown eyes. He saw the muzzle of my equalizer, then dropped the blade. "Eek!" The blade bounced a couple of times. It was rubber. Bruce stood shaking; hands over his eyes. "It's just my costume, Mr. Harlow. Please don't hurt me."

I replaced my heater, then retrieved Bruce's rubber sword and handed it to him. "Here, kid. I didn't mean to scare you. You kind of startled me, that's all."

". . . just a costume." Bruce was sobbing. Pitiful. I reached out a hand and patted him on the shoulder.

"Look, kid, it's all right --" Bruce's shoulder fell off and bounced a couple of times. More rubber. I handed him back his shoulder. "Here, kid. Pull yourself together."

script. For longer works (mailed in boxes) paper clip the proper postage to the cover letter. If your manuscript is being submitted in a country other than your own, enclose International Reply Coupons or an International Money Order of the proper amount instead of stamps (the coupons can be picked up at any post office). After a manuscript has been around a few times, it will look dirty, beat up, and rejected. Submit a new copy, or at least repair your current copy.

COVER LETTERS

What is the purpose of a cover letter? If an established writer is approaching a new editor, the cover letter is used to list a few professional publishing credits in the way of an introduction. If you are submitting a manuscript in response to an editor's favorable reaction to your query, the cover letter is used as a reminder that your manuscript is not unsolicited. If the editor is an old friend, the cover letter might be used as an opportunity to say "Hi!" If you are a beginner, what is a cover letter for? All you can say in it is "Here's my manuscript," and the editor already knows that, provided that you remembered to enclose your manuscript. But I have been at the slushpile, and it is remarkable what beginners use cover letters for.

A frequent kind of cover letter is the one laying out the demands the author expects in payment for the story, the rights to be negotiated, what artist should illustrate the piece, down to and including the issue in which the story should appear. The speed at which those manuscripts return to their senders would have Einstein believing in FTL travel.

Another, more frequent, kind of letter is the "take pity on me" variety. "I'm just starting in writing, and I don't think you will like this story, but I thought I'd send it along so you can tell me what's wrong with it. P.S. My mother is dying from cancer . . . ." Into the chute with that one too. If the author doesn't believe in the story any more than that, why should the editor?

Then there is Chatty Chatty Bang Bang: the beginner who has nothing to say, but feels obligated to fill out a letter-sized sheet because someone said there has to be a cover letter. What then follows covers the range from life histories to backyard gossip and regional sagas. A variation on this is the "Oracle of Things To Come." A beginner who has nothing to say, hence he or she takes up a page or two talking about the story that came with the letter, thereby giving the editor the not too welcome task of reading the same story twice.

There are others of interest: those who relate in certain terms how stupid the editor is if the manuscript is not purchased; threats to commit suicide if another rejection is seen; persons of "influence" who will have the editor's job upon getting a "no sale," and so on.

Two things to keep in mind about cover letters: first, if you don't have anything to say, don't feel obligated to send a cover letter; second, if you do send a cover letter, remember that it is an example of your writing ability and it will be the first thing the editor will see—and judge.

I have been told that your story won't be hurt by a bad cover letter; but it certainly won't be helped. Therefore, the letter should (1) have a purpose, and (2) be well written. Again, stay away from weird stationery—particularly if it is perfumed. There's nothing that brightens up the office on a hot summer day quite so much as a manuscript that literally stinks before it is opened.

COPYREADING AND REVISION FORMATS

No matter how hard you try, that final draft will have errors in it. Typos, misspelled words, a scene that needs rewriting, another scene that needs throwing out, and so on. And there are ways to indicate corrections standard to the profession. If it is necessary, for example, to add a page between pages 45 and 46, number the new page 45A. If it is necessary to delete two pages between page numbers 30 and 33, insert a blank sheet between 30 and 33 and number the sheet 31-32. This saves renumbering a long manuscript and will not confuse the typesetter. For short manuscripts, renumber the entire thing. (Fig. 9/5)

PROOFREADING

With typeset copy, things are much more cramped. About all you can do is indicate where the problem is, then state the correction in the margin. A caution: do not use this opportunity for rewriting. Not only is it expensive, *you* may be the one paying the tab. Book contracts are very clear about this point. (Pg. 152)

ON PICKING NITS

In reviewing draft copies of *SFWW-I*, some people pointed out to me several times that certain things—such as what symbol to use for scene breaks, header format, the direction of addresses on envelopes, the quality of cover letters—are not big deals. No one is going to reject your story because of a dirty mailing envelope, for example. This is true. Editors are not eighth-grade English teachers (well, most of them aren't). Any one of the little details mentioned above, not observed, will not mean an automatic rejection. Then why spend a chapter nitpicking?

Between writing a story and putting it in proper manuscript form, there is an incredible number of detail things to do. The greater number of those details that you get right, the greater become your chances of a sale. Format, spelling, page and mailer cleanliness are small things—nits—by themselves. But they are signals to the editor that you take what you are doing seriously—professionally.

However, if you combine all of those nits and do them wrong—filthy hand-addressed mailer (postage due), no return envelope, manuscript typed in faded green ribbon on "easy erase" paper, filthy type in all upper case, no margins, pages misnumbered, corrections unreadable in addition to using the wrong symbols, scene breaks indicated by triple-asterisks—your story still might not be rejected. However, if purchased, it will probably be given to a grownup to put into manuscript form, which will probably come out of your check. As is true for you, your typewriter has only one asterisk; save it for something special.

COPYREADING SYMBOLS

The winds of the planet Viula
were harsh, never ending entities,
fleeing from the globe's death cold
poles to meet and crash at the equator
where Viula's dim sun would warm them,
sending them screaming back the sto\
coldness. The rock and ice of the planet
showed paths carved there by the winds. The
last snow on viula fell long ago, before
the coldness came, when there was warmth
enough for water to evaporate.

In the night skys sharp clearness,
stars burned the blackness twinkling

Make paragraph

Insert word & comma

Insert hyphen

Correct spelling

Delete word & close up

Transpose words

Delete words & connect

Use capitals

Use lower case

Insert space

Insert apostrophe*

Insert comma*

CHAPTER NINE

as the waves of ~~driving~~ wind blew. *stet.*   Cancel correction; let original version stand**

The planet's moon rose from the   Insert scene break

horizon purple and airless. "Margo, is   Insert long dash

that you? Al walked the rim of the   Insert closing quote***

crater. Margo, where're you at?" He   Insert opening quote***

stopped and stared. "Margo. Is that   Use italics

you?" Robot DDABNA looked over Al's   Use small capitals

shoulder   Insert period

"That's Margo, all right," it said.   Use bold face

    No paragraph; go on to next page****

*Note difference. Use ⌄ to indicate missing letters: "Sho 'nuff?"
**Use to cancel a correction and for strange spellings: "spellerings."
***Note difference. Typesetter's quotation marks, are polarized.
****Do not end every page in this manner. Use only when ending a page short at the end of a sentence in the middle of a paragraph.

PROOFREADING SYMBOLS

sighed as the weight was removed from his legs. "I'm afraid I'm not used to this all walking." **Delete letter & close up**

Close up

Transpose words

Sanford grinned. "One of those ivory tower boys, eh Rawls?" **Cancel correction; let stand** STET

Insert comma

Rawls smiled sheepishly. "I suppose I am. Theory interests me, but application leaves me rather cold. i suppose it's different with you fliers?" **Make paragraph**

Use lower case

Use capitals cap

Put in italics /Ital

Sanford nodded "My meat is action; philosophy in action. He shrugged. "I don't suppose that we contribute as much to the dishiplyne as the theoreticians, but we do make philosophy viable in the marketplace, don't we? If SHAWNA didn't bring in all those nice green passenger credits, who would finance the theoreticians? I ask you." **Insert period**

Insert closing quote

Insert apostrophe

Correct spelling /discipline

Use even spacing eq#

Use small caps sc

Replace damaged type

Delete hyphen & leave space

Insert space /#

"Your point is well-taken, Captain." Rawls twiddled his thumbs for a bit. "Captain Sanford, a semanticist I am aware of the vast distance between the-ory and practice. Yet Doctor Veggnitz has given me quite a handsome fee to **Insert hyphen**

Take out words

Insert word & space #as#

Correct hyphenation

Align theo=/ry

Note the difference between the apostrophe and the comma. Also note the difference between an opening quotation mark and a closing quotation mark. When in doubt about what symbol or combination of symbols to use, spell out the correct version in the margin.

REFERENCES

For a thorough reference list, covering representative fiction works in SF and fantasy, bibliographies, nonfiction works in both genres, as well as reference works in science, history, and technology, see *Science Fiction Handbook Revised,* by L. Sprague de Camp and Catherine C. de Camp (Owlswick Press, Philadelphia, 1975). For those interested in writing science fiction, teaching SF, or teaching SF writing, the references cited in this volume are unexcelled.

Since I began writing, I have found a number of things of value in learning my craft and advancing in it. It covers such a wide range of literature that it would be impossible to list everything. However, for day to day use, I find the following indispensable:

Follett's Vest Pocket 50,000 Words, by Harry Sharp (Follett, 1964). This is a collection of words, spelled and divided, and without definitions. I once used it in typesetting, and it serves the same purpose in writing: a speedy way to find the correct spelling of a word without having to juggle eight pounds of dictionary.

Roget's Thesaurus in Dictionary Form, edited by Norman Lewis (Putnam's, 1964). Remember Mark Twain's dictum: "Use the right word, not its second cousin." Looking for a different word because you have used the word "bright" seven times in the last paragraph? This is the place to go. Looking for new synonyms for "he said"? Don't.

Bartlett's Familiar Quotations, whatever edition. Bartlett's is a shortcut to most of the memorable things that have ever been said or written. Use it as an index through which great works and themes can be explored. It is also a terrific source of titles. I also have *The Oxford Dictionary of Quotations, 3rd Ed., (Oxford University Press, Oxford, 1979).* Both works accomplish about the same thing, the Oxford work being possibly more current and easier on the eyes.

The current *World Almanac & Book of Facts.* Not only can any two things from this volume produce a story idea, it can save you from getting yards of misinformation. I have a set of similar references that goes back to 1904. The current one is on your newsstand; the old ones can be picked up at used book stores and flea markets.

National Geographic Magazine. My set of *Geographics* is complete back to the year 1941, and I have the index to all of those issues (available from the National Geographic Society). Pick your time, your setting: this publication has probably done one or more articles on it, with pictures. Again, used book stores and flea markets. A subscription wouldn't hurt.

Science News. A weekly publication that informs you on the latest developments in the world of science. When an issue shows up, I browse through it, then file it. *Science News* publishes periodic indices, and when a story comes up, it is a simple matter to run through the index and pick out whatever anyone has said or done recently in a particular field.

Van Nostrand's Scientific Encyclopedia edited by Douglas M. Considine (Van Nostrand Reinhold, fifth edition, 1976). My background is in the "soft sciences," and I don't know a compandor from a commutator. This volume supplies me with enough information on any scientific topic to enable me to decide whether I want to mess with it or not.

Great Books of the Western World edited by Robert Maynard Hutchins (Encyclopaedia Britannica, 1952). Fifty-four volumes of literature, history, science, and philosophy from Homer to Freud, indexed, introduced, and cross-referenced. This set is twenty-five hundred years of human discussion and thought on virtually every issue that has ever interested, tickled, or plagued humanity.

Encyclopaedia Britannica. I have the fourteenth edition (1929) and the fifteenth edition (1974). This lets me explore everything (to 1974) and what we thought it was fifty years ago. If this doesn't satiate my curiosity on a particular subject, the references at the ends of the articles show me where to go for more.

The American Heritage Dictionary of the English Language. There is more fuss over dictionaries than one would believe. I also have the *Oxford English Dictionary,* just in case I want to enter a doctoral program on a particular word. *The American College Dictionary* has one small problem: too few words. I donated my copy to a church book sale. The *Heritage* dictionary has most of the words, and is very generous with the spellings of the different tenses. In addition, it is in a single volume that won't crowd out your desk.

The references above are my daily working tools. To collect all of them today would be expensive, but the desk *has* to have the dictionary and the thesaurus. If you can't spell, you also need the *50,000 Words.* The rest can be found in any good library. The books listed below are useful to varying degrees.

The Elements of Style by William Strunk and E. B. White (Macmillan, 1979). This volume (very tiny) has nothing whatever to do with style, but it is the only sane book on English usage and grammar ever written. It should be memorized.

Notes to a Science Fiction Writer by Ben Bova (Scribners, 1975). In this volume, Bova uses some of his own stories in combination with discussions on the mechanics of writing. The discussions will add depth to your knowledge of how different writers write. So will the stories.

Science Fiction Handbook, Revised by L. Sprague & Catherine C. de Camp (Owlswick Press, 1975). This book is one of the more readable overviews of the profession of writing science fiction and fantasy. It will add to your depth of how it is done by others.

The Craft of Science Fiction edited by Reginald Bretnor (Harper & Row, 1976). This work answers many questions about the trade and will expose you to a still wider range of writing approaches and techniques.

The S.F.W.A. Handbook edited by Mildred Downey Broxon (Science Fiction Writers of America, 1976). This thing is probably the most ineptly printed and bound volume since Gutenberg; however, it is crowded with tips, advice, instruction, references, and other good stuff.

Of Worlds Beyond edited by Lloyd Arthur Eshback (Advent, 1964). A bit outdated, but valuable for the peeks it gives you into other writers' heads.

The Science Fiction Encyclopedia edited by Peter Nichols (Doubleday, 1979). A good guide to the who, what, and where of science fiction.

TERMS

BACKFILL—Devices for explaining the existence or nature of a prior event or situation.

BAT DURSTON—A story set in a science fiction future that can be translated line-for-line into a Western with six-guns instead of blasters, etc. A variation of this is the Batgard Durstonwolfe, where the story can be translated into a sword-swinging Viking saga. Space opera, perhaps; but not science fiction.

BRIGHT MOMENT—A moment within the story buildup when, to the character in its struggle to achieve its goal, it appears that all obstacles have been overcome.

BUILDUP—The events in a story that transpire between the introduction of the problem and the story's climax.

CHANGE—The emotional-intellectual alteration of a story character through the events that take place within a story.

CHARACTER(S)—The being(s) that populate stories.

CHARACTERIZATION—The investment of qualities (looks, strengths, weaknesses, goals) into a character such that those qualities can be perceived by the reader.

CHARACTER SITUATION—The character in its setting facing the main story conflict determined by the character's goals and the obstacle(s) in the path of the achievement of those goals.

CHEAP ENDING—Also called an "easy ending." As in: "Then I woke up—and it had all been nothing but a dream!" The chief result of cheap endings is to leave the reader unsatisfied.

CHEATING (the reader)—Withholding information that should not be withheld, such as that the protagonist is a giant lobster. At *IA'sfm* this is called the "Tomato Surprise." A variation of this is trying to create an aura of "mystery" or "artsiness" by failing to state the story situation at the beginning with sufficient clarity, or by leaving out pertinent facts.

CLIMAX—That moment following the buildup in a story usually containing the action that resolves the story's main conflict.

CONFLICT—Opposition to the achievement or maintenance of a goal.

CONFUSING—The reader (editor) is in doubt as to what is going on, where it is happening, why it is happening (motivation), and so on. "Murky" is a more extreme condemnation, while "Opaque" is the ultimate expression of being totally lost in a story.

CONSISTENCY— As with the world of reality, the world of unreality that you create must be consistent. If flipping switch 2 to position 3 in Chapter One causes plague to be released, then it better do the same thing in Chapter Five unless the switch has been rewired. Consider this: even in fantasy, the premise of "no rules" is a rule. Consistency with that rule must be maintained to maintain reader plausibility.

CONTENT—The ideas, morals, characters, problems, conflicts, conflict resolutions, and purposes within a story. "Lack of content" can mean that either the idea or underlying message is trivial, the story has no point, it's not about anything, or it doesn't do anything.

COPYEDITING—In the publishing operation, the copyeditor is the person who reads the story in manuscript form to catch all the mistakes the author didn't catch. In both copyediting and author's minor corrections, the same symbols are used.

CUTESY, THE CUTES—A condemnation of story treatment meaning that the story seems written more toward four-year-old children than adults. "The cutes" are difficult to define, and almost impossible for the author to detect until an editor points it out. From the editor's point of view (and from the reader's) the characters are sugary, goody goody, syrupy and/or "just too dear for words." Watch out for the cutes when the characters in your story are children, R2D2 type robots, or fuzzy little aliens.

CUTTING—Reducing the word length of a story. Sometimes this is done because of a publication's space limitations; but it is done more often to remove from a piece unnecessary wordage.

DARK MOMENT—That moment when a character's plans all appear to have failed, leaving the character in worse trouble than when the story began.

DESCRIPTION—Narrative or dialog relating the nature of the properties of something, someone, or someplace.

DEUS EX MACHINA—"God from a Machine." In Greek and Roman drama, when the writer of the script had worked his characters into an impossible situation, a mythical god brought on stage by machinery intervened and untangled the plot. Since then, "deus ex machina" and "the long arm of coincidence," have become the terms used to indicate any improbable character, event, device, or circumstance suddenly introduced into a story to resolve a situation.

DIALECT—Spelling the words in quoted conversation in a fashion designed to reflect a regional variation of a language or an accent.

DIALOG—The words spoken or thought by a character or characters within a story.

DOWN—Sad, unpleasing, depressing. A down story is one with a negative view and an unhappy or tragic ending.

DRAGGING (the story)—Where the author takes an incomplete idea—perhaps the beginning, middle, or end of a story—and begins writing, forcing the remainder of the idea to produce itself upon the paper.

DRAGGING (the author)—Where a character in a story decides to go in a direction different than that chosen by the author.

DREAM SEQUENCE—a scene consisting of a viewpoint character's dream.

FANTASY—Fiction built on mythology. Fantasy is based on or contains magic as magic; gods, sorcerers, witches, etc., with powers that work; ghosts, demons, werewolves, vampires of the Dracula persuasion, and the like.

FLASHBACK—a form of backfill that brings the reader from one scene to a chronologically previous scene.

FLESHING OUT—Adding words to a story to make it more effective, such as by continuing themes, adding needed description, tying up loose ends, etc. Not to be confused with padding.

FLUFF—Bad: stories of little content. Good: light entertaining humor.

FRAME—One or more scenes, or an entire story, used as a setting for the main story.

FUTILITY—The story has no point, except possibly that the world is cruel, in trouble, difficult or impossible to understand, and full of injustices.

GALLEYS—Copies of typeset material used for proofreading and indicating needed corrections.

GAP—A confusing jump from one situation, premise, brand of logic, viewpoint, etc. to another. For example, Garballs is fleeing from his enemies upon a twelve-legged Snorth before a scene break and is in the cockpit of a starcruiser after the break with no explanation about whence the ship came.

GREENER'S LAW—"Never argue with a man who buys ink by the barrel."

HOOK—A story opening that captures the reader's attention sufficiently to cause him to move on to the next paragraph.

IDENTIFICATION—The reader—to a degree—"becoming" one of the characters in a story.

IGNORANT DEVICE—Ways of having a character within the story state something that the author wishes the reader to know without requiring another character in the scene. Two examples of ignorant devices are voice logs and voice input computers.

KENT COUNTY SYNDROME—Giving the reader the feel that the entire planet upon which the story is set is no larger and no more varied than Kent County, Delaware.

LECTURE—A form of dialog or narration in a story where the author attempts to establish something either by having a character blather on for line after eternal line, or by using the narration of the story to deliver an essay to the reader.

LIMERICK—A form of verse perverse.

> A limerick's a verse with a rhyme.
> Its style nowhere else can you find;
>   I would tell you much more,
>   But I've only sold four,
> To the rest SF's not been too kind.

LOOSE END—An unresolved conflict, problem, or issue within a story.

MOTIVATION—The determinants causing a character's behavior.

MS(S)—Manuscript(s).

MULTIPLE SUBMISSION—The practice of submitting copies of the same work to more than one editor at a time. Do *not* make multiple submissions to magazines; they're too much bother and will be rejected. If you are doing a multiple submission to a book house, be certain to inform the editors of this fact in your cover letters.

NOLAN'S OBSERVATION—"The difference between smart people and dumb people isn't that smart people don't make mistakes. They just don't keep making the same mistake over and over again."

OBSTACLE—That which stands in the path to a character's goals.

OUTLINE—A skeletal version of a story that serves as a plan by working out in advance the major characters, plot, and points of action.

PADDING—Adding words unnecessary to a story to increase its length.

PARALLEL RUNNING SCENES—a form of backfill that takes a separate story, or a scene, and intersperses it in parts throughout the main story to explain or illustrate the events taking place in the main story.

PLANT—Narration, dialog, or description placed in the body of a story to prepare the reader for something that will happen later in the story that would be otherwise implausible, unconvincing, or misunderstood.

PLOT—The total of the events that take place in a story.

PREDICTABLE—The story is presented in such a manner that the reader can too easily guess the outcome of a conflict or the ending of a story long before it is unfolded by the author.

PREQUEL—A condition descriptive of baby porcupines before they grow their protective coats; also used to describe a story written after the story it is before.

PROOFREADING—The process of reading and correcting galleys. Because of space limitations with set type, proofreading symbols and methods are different from those for copyediting.

PROPOSAL—An offer to an editor to write a specific work. Proposals are usually required only for novel-length works or nonfiction pieces, and are acceptable (usually) only from writers the editor knows well. The usual proposal consists of an outline of the proposed work, in addition to one or two completed chapters for a novel-length work to show the editor the intended treatment of the material.

PSEUDONYMS, PEN NAMES—A name other than the author's real name.

PUN—Beats me; but then, knowbody's perfect.

QUERY—A brief note asking an editor if he or she would be interested in seeing your proposal or completed manuscript. If the work is lengthy, a query can save you some postage; only pay the single ounce rate to obtain your "not interested." Enclose SASE. If the editor *is* interested, your manuscript is no longer "unsolicited," and you should mention this in your cover letter.

RESOLUTION—The outcome of or solution to the problems and/or conflicts raised within a story.

REFERENCE—A form of backfill that explains current situations through dialog referring to the reasons leading up to the situation. A caution: do not take up story space having characters explain to each other what they (in the story) already know.

SASE—Self Addressed Stamped Envelope.

SATIRE—Witty, entertaining works (that sell) that make sport of revered persons or institutions; to be distinguished from "bad taste," which doesn't sell.

SCENE—A subdivision of a story which constitutes a unit of continuous related action.

SCENE BREAK—The skipping of an extra line to indicate a scene change in a story. Scene breaks are inserted to indicate changes in time, location, viewpoint, etc. In manuscript form, a scene break is indicated by centering the number sign, #, in the skipped line. The # in the center of a line indicates to the typesetter that an extra line space is to be inserted at that point.

SCITHERS'S SOLACE—"Editors don't reject people; they reject pieces of paper." LONGYEAR'S LAMENT—"There is no way not to take a rejection personally." SCITHERS'S REJOINDER—"I know; but pretend you don't." LONGYEAR'S CAPITULATION—"%$#&3-@*!!."

SEAMS—Letting where the parts of a story join together show.

SETTING—The location in time and space of a scene.

SLOW—The number of words in the story per significant event taking place is too high.

SMOKE—Good: with each reading the story reveals new things. Bad: something is wrong with the story, but the editor doesn't know what.

SPEC—Short for "speculation." Writing and submitting a manuscript with no editorial assurances of a sale.

SPEECH TAGS—Devices used to indicate which character is speaking.

SLUSHPILE—The daily load of unsolicited manuscripts that must be waded through by an editor or reader to find your gem.

SUCKING IN (The reader)—A process of leading the reader into buying your insane premise or situation by placing the viewpoint character into an acceptable situation, then bit by bit, replacing the parts of that situation by swallowable bites until the reader has eaten the whole thing.

TIGHTEN UP—To take the wandering around out of a scene or story; getting from A to B by a more direct route.

TRAGEDY—a story in which the protagonist does not achieve his goals, or if the goals are achieved, the achievement brings unexpected grief. A tragedy can be either serious, humorous, or both.

TRAILER—A brief scene following the climax of a story.

TRANSITIONS—Devices for moving from one scene, viewpoint character, or situation to another without losing the reader.

TRUCK ENDINGS—Endings that are not the believable consequence of the events that transpired within the story ("and then everybody got run over by a truck").

UFO—Unidentified Flying Objects. Leave them that way.

UP—Happy, pleasing and/or satisfying. An up story is one with a positive view and a happy ending.

VIEWPOINT—The "eyes" through which the happenings in the story are seen.

VIEWPOINT CHARACTER—The character through whose eyes the story is seen.

VIEWPOINT SHIFTING—Changing from one viewpoint character to another.

VIGNETTE—"Snapshot," character study, or "slice-of-life" type works.

WORKSHOP SUGGESTIONS

This book can be used in a variety of workshop formats. With a one-session science fiction convention workshop, the concentration should be on Chapter One to get those attending familiar with both the parts of a story and with story diagramming. Since there will be a ready supply of writers at SF cons, you might devote a portion of the workshop to diagramming, analyzing, and generally tearing up a professional writer's story—with the author sitting there. During question and answer time, the author can explain, or try to explain, the reasons for how and why the story was written. *Do not* take a beginner's story and rip it up. First, you won't have the time; second, it will not be productive.

A two-session convention workshop (and tell the committee to schedule the sessions as far apart as possible) can cover a lot of territory. This book is brief enough to be read in an hour or two, allowing those attending the workshop to attend the second session having read it and having completed some of the exercises. Devote the first session to Chapter One, again concentrating on the parts of a story, story diagramming, and analysis. At the end of the session, assign the reading of the book, and the analysis of one or more of the stories in Chapter Seven. At the second session, diagram and discuss the stories assigned for analysis. With those attending the workshop having this experience, the second session is a good place to schedule the author whose story you wish to broil.

Week-long, "colony" type workshops can begin with Chapter One. Assign the reading of the book and the diagramming and analysis of one or more of the stories in Chapter Seven. Follow this with exercises and discussions from Chapters Two and Three. Perhaps as much as half of a week-long workshop can be then devoted to having the attendees apply what they have learned to stories of their own. Have them diagram and analyze one or more of their own stories. Longer workshops (two and three weeks) enable those attending to analyze their stories, and then rewrite where needed.